Remembering
Nigeria

An Autobiography

by
Everett L. Phillips

Foreword by J. Philip Hogan
Epilogue by Rex Jackson
Farewell by Charles O. Osueke
Adapted by Louise Jeter Walker

ISBN 0-8297-6700-2

a 1989 by Life Publishers International
    3360 N.W. 110th St., Miami, Florida 33167

Cover design by John Coté

*Dedicated to
all the missionaries
— and their children —
who have consecrated their lives
to the great and wonderful task
of bringing the Gospel of Jesus Christ
to all Nigerians*

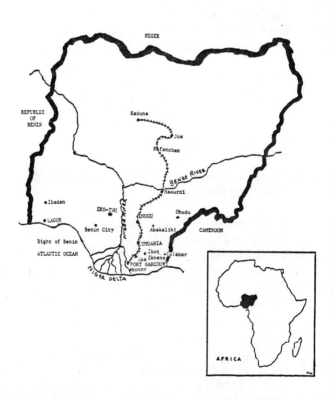

Contents

Foreword

"According to the grace of God which was given to me, as a wise master builder I have laid the foundation, and another builds on it. But let each one take heed how he builds on it." 1 Corinthians 3:10.

This book is about fundamentals like building and foundations — about training and discipling at the earliest stages of the development of a church on the mission field. It's about line upon line, and precept upon precept, preparing the national workers and the national church for leadership. It's an example of how, for three quarters of a century, we Assemblies of God people have sought to do missionary work.

It puts the emphasis where it belongs — on people, their call, their commitment, and their continuity in the work of God. It's about good, godly, wholesome people who left an indelible mark on Africa in general and on West Africa and Nigeria in particular.

Finally, it exemplifies the value of a sense of humor that allows a person to look upon challenges, problems, and obstacles as passing experiences. As I dictate these lines, memories of the years I was associated with Everett Phillips come flooding back — his hearty laughter booming down the halls, the smile with which he met me every workday.

You will share in his laughter and tears as you read the experiences of Nigerians and missionaries who accepted God's call and met the challenge. Through a life-

time of service they contributed to one of the great revival
movements of West Africa.

Philip Hogan
Executive Director of Foreign Missions

Acknowledgements

I am deeply indebted to many whose encouragement, assistance, and prayers have made this book possible:

To Dorothy, my beloved wife, whose devotion to the call of God and constant encouragement and help have made this book possible.

To Lloyd Shirer, my friend who introduced us to Africa. To George Alioha, who wrote *The History of the Assemblies of God in Nigeria.* To Rex Jackson and Elmer Frink, loyal friends who lived many of these experiences with us and had a part in this story. To Kenneth Godbey, whose experiences in Eastern Nigeria are legendary.

To Ralph Cimino, who contributed information on the recent history of the growth of the Assemblies of God in Nigeria. To Adele Dalton for providing source material and encouragement. To Lynn Wertz and Beatrice Craft for transcribing tapes. And to Alma Smith for her many hours of editing, rewriting, and typing.

Most of all, I am thankful to God for the outpouring of His Holy Spirit upon a small group of believers to bring to birth the robust church that is working in His Nigerian vineyard today.

Editor's Note: This book represents Everett Phillips' final earthly labor of love for the Lord and His church. We thank all who, after his death, have helped with pictures and in other ways to prepare the manuscript for publication in the States and Nigeria.

CHAPTER ONE

To Go or Not to Go?

Did God Really Call Us?

Donald, Dorothy, and Everett Phillips, 1939

"It doesn't look like we're going to make it!" I told my wife, Dorothy. "We have either been the wrong people or have applied at the wrong time. We've tried four times to go somewhere, anywhere, in Africa."

We had heard of the need for a couple in the Belgian Congo. I called the Foreign Missions Director of the Assemblies of God, offering to go, but was told the need had already been met. We were not needed! Since our youth we had felt God's to go to Africa. And now I was already older than the age at which missionaries were usually appointed. Would we ever be able to go?

After a long silence Dorothy answered quietly, "Everett, to tell you the truth, I never felt that God wanted us in the Congo. Remember we have been praying for years for God's will. Each time we applied for missionary service, the door has definitely closed. Let's leave it that way. When it is His time, He will open the door for us. For now, let's just stay in our church in Alton and do what He's called us to do for the moment — pastor the church God has given us."

"We'll do it," I replied.

In the following months God blessed our church, and we became deeply involved in the district work of the Assemblies of God in Illinois. But always the nagging question was in our minds: Did God really call us to Africa? Or was it just our imagination? And if He called us, why all these years of delay? Was this just a delay, or did God intend for us to continue our pastoral work and forget about missionary work? For years Africa had been foremost in our minds.

For me, it all began when I was a boy. Part of my early training came in hearing missionaries tell about God's guidance in the great work of winning converts and establishing churches. Africa held a special appeal for me. My father was interested in Africa. He loved to read, and I read the same books he did. These included fascinating stories about Africa.

Every year a number of missionaries came to our church for a missionary convention. The pastor, knowing our family's interest in Africa, had the missionaries to Africa stay in our home. I would sit in awe, listening to them talk and learning what it meant to be an African missionary. God used these experiences to help form a dream in my heart.

As the years passed, I knew that some day I would be

a preacher and perhaps even a missionary to Africa.

God led me to Central Bible Institute to prepare for the ministry. On Friday afternoons the students met in groups to pray for various areas of the world. For three years I attended the African prayer group and learned about the field, the missionaries, and needs.

Meanwhile, I had fallen in love with Dorothy Prohaska, a girl from my home church in Cleveland, Ohio. When I first met Dorothy, her feet couldn't reach the floor when she sat on a church pew. We both grew up in church, so I knew her very well. She became an usherette in the church, and the church pianist.

God had been dealing with Dorothy too about Africa. During my third year of Bible school she became a first-year student. We were very interested in each other, but I thought I needed to become a self-supporting pastor before I could ask her to marry me.

After graduating in 1928 I did evangelistic work and church-planting, then became the pastor of a small church in Galesburg, Illinois — letting the people know that I expected to go to Africa as soon as God opened the door. Meanwhile, Dorothy graduated and was taking nurses' training. We were married in 1932.

We were supremely happy at God's goodness to us, for we had a home, a church, and soon would be on our way to Africa (or so we thought). Sometimes after laying aside our tithes, rent, and utility money, we had less than a dollar for food, and no transportation except our feet. But somehow God met our needs and we helped others. Good preparation for the mission field!

In our third year there our church held its first missionary convention. The executive director of the Foreign Missions Department, Noel Perkin, was our speaker. We talked with him about our call to Africa. He wisely advised us to wait for God's time and His special guidance. Since there was no opening for us at that time, we waited and prayed month after month.

The church grew and so did our family. When our son Donald was born, Dorothy had a serious problem and for hours was at the point of death. But God gave her the assurance of Psalm 91. Afterwards she referred to it repeatedly as her very special promise from God.

But the years were passing; we had diligently prepared ourselves to be missionaries, but no door opened. Africa seemed farther away than ever before. Had we been mistaken about the call?

A Door to Nigeria?

In February 1939 something happened to revive our hopes at the District Ministers' Institute. Rev. J.R. Flower, secretary of the General Council, gave a glowing report about the churches in Africa. He and Noel Perkin had just visited the work there.

On their journey they went through customs in Lagos, Nigeria. In this office were some Ibo tribesmen. When they learned that the visitors were American ministers, they told them of a great revival in their area and asked if they were familiar with an experience called "the baptism in the Holy Spirit." When Brother Flower and Brother Perkin said they had received this experience, the Ibo men were overjoyed and pleaded with them to visit Eastern Nigeria.

Some followed them to their hotel to talk more about their wonderful experiences. One of the hotel employees brought them a copy of the *Pentecostal Evangel*. "Do you know this paper?" he asked.

In reply, Brother Flower turned to the list of names of the officials of the General Council and pointed out his and Noel Perkin's names. They explained that the magazine was the official publication of their church, the Assemblies of God.

That settled it. The men insisted, "You must send missionaries to us; we need help." The next morning a group of believers escorted them to the ship that would take them back to America. Again they pleaded, "Please send us missionaries."

After relating this experience, Brother Flower made an appeal for young people to go to Nigeria.

I waited two days before asking Dorothy: "What do you think about Nigeria?" Her answer was evasive. She didn't seem ready to speak about the need in Nigeria.

One week later I was reading in the *Pentecostal Evangel* about a great revival in Nigeria when Dorothy came to the study and said: "I can't go on this way any longer. I must talk about this matter of Nigeria. I have never told you this, but God called me to Nigeria when I received the Holy Spirit."

Then she told about a vision God had given her when she was baptized in the Holy Spirit. He showed her the coast of West Africa with its big hump and river that runs south to the ocean. She saw herself ministering to women along the shore of that great waterway.

Jennie Carlson, a returned missionary from Liberia, was praying with Dorothy and the other young people who were receiving the baptism in the Spirit. Dorothy asked her: "Jennie, what is the name of the river that runs straight south from the Sahara Desert to the ocean?" She drew a little outline map of Africa to show Jennie the location of the river.

Jennie answered, "Dorothy, that's the Niger River. It flows through Nigeria. But, Dorothy, they have had the Word of God there for almost 100 years. I don't think we will ever send missionaries to Nigeria." She said this with sympathy for Dorothy, feeling she might be misled by the vision and discouraged later if the way was not open for her to go there.

So, Dorothy decided, "Lord, if this is real, I'll obey

You. But You must deal with this problem. If I'm ever to go to Africa, I'd like to go to Nigeria." She didn't tell even her mother about it. She had never told me, even though we had been married seven years and had talked often about going to Africa. I knew she was willing to go, there was no hesitancy about that, but she had never talked about Nigeria. She was afraid to, because Jennie had said it was a country to which our church would probably never send missionaries.

Now we had heard from Brother Flower about the immediate need for help in Nigeria. As she told me the whole story, we wept together and prayed, as we had done many times before. But this time it was different, for it seemed that at long last God was doing something of which we had never dreamed.

That afternoon I called Brother Perkin and said we had heard about the need in Nigeria and that Dorothy and I were still very much interested in Africa. We offered to meet with the Missions Committee if they would receive us. "By all means come, and we will talk about it," Brother Perkin replied.

What Would the Committee Decide?

Never will I forget meeting with the Missions Committee! We explained that we had been trying to go to Africa, as they knew, for years. Now I was 35 years old. If I were ever going, it would have to be soon, before I was too old. "Do you think there is an opportunity for us in Nigeria?" I asked.

"Brother Phillips," they said, "perhaps God has been in this. You have been active in your district, holding various offices, helping in building and starting churches, supervising various areas of the work of God in Illinois. Perhaps He has been preparing you for this very day! For this work in Nigeria, if we can believe all we hear, is in need of someone with special experience in how to set up an organization, someone who can organize churches so that they will build on the right foundation for years to come."

After further discussion they told us: "We feel this is of God." All the delays of the past had been of God's leading up to this very moment as they appointed us to Nigeria, West Africa. Only then did Dorothy share with them the story of her call to Nigeria.

On Our Way!

The next Sunday morning I read my resignation to our church, explaining that God had opened the door for us to go to Nigeria. In May, Dorothy was ordained to the ministry at the District Council. We had been stopped from going to Africa until God's time came, and then every door was opened. He provided for every need.

In November, 1939, we went to New York expecting to sail in a week on the Queen Mary. But just then the war broke out in Europe. Shipping was disrupted. The Queen Mary was to stay in New York indefinitely. Surely the Lord wouldn't bring us this far and then close the door, would He?

After a month's stay in New York, we went to Lisbon, Portugal, on an Italian ship, and then on a Dutch ship down the West coast of Africa. God was with us!

Five Dutch ships had left Rotterdam at the beginning of the war; four were sunk by German submarines between Rotterdam and Lisbon, leaving only one ship, the Amstelkerk. It was to take us to Nigeria.

In those days Holland was trying to declare her neutrality, so a Dutch flag 100 feet long was painted on each side of the ship. Floodlights illuminated the flag and the whole ship. This declared its neutrality, but also made it a wonderful target for submarines!

On the Amstelkerk 28 missionaries were traveling to West Africa. The captain constantly warned us of dangers.

Dutch ships were being sunk all around the world. We were to sleep in our clothes with our passports and money with us. God kept us and gave us an interesting, month-long trip to Nigeria.

CHAPTER TWO

Africa at Last!

Home Sweet Home

Nigeria at last! What boundless joy Dorothy and I had as our ship entered the Bonny River, part of the mouth of the great Niger River! Hundreds of small canoes piled high with unbelievable loads hurried to get away from the waves caused by our ship's bow. Port Harcourt, 70 miles upriver, *was our destination.* Our hearts overflowed with thanksgiving. Our prayers were being fulfilled! Our 5-year-old Don saw us laughing and crying and wondered at our strange actions.

There is nothing beautiful about the mud flats of the Niger Delta, but to us everything was beautiful — it was Nigeria! After years of hoping, praying, despairing, we had reached the land of our calling, the land that was to be our home for many years.

When the ship docked, words can't describe our feelings as Lloyd and Margaret Shirer (missionaries to the Gold Coast) and the pastor and members of the Port Harcourt church gave us a warm welcome.

The Shirers, at Noel Perkin's suggestion, had checked out the reports of the revival in Eastern Nigeria, ministered in the churches, organized the work, and were there to help us get settled.

The Shirers took us to the one-room house, with a veranda on three sides, that they had rented for us. They would be staying with us for six months, until we knew

our way around and learned a few of the lessons that
every new missionary needs to know.

They helped us make our new home as bug-proof and
mosquito-proof as possible. We screened the veranda,
and the Shirers used it for bedroom, dining room and
living room. Margaret and Dorothy made mosquito nets
for our beds, because in spite of screening, mosquitos still
got into the house. Malaria was common; and the carrier,
the anopheles mosquito, was ever present.

"Sir, Is This True?"

Our first Sunday in Port Harcourt, Lloyd preached in
the morning service, and I in the evening. Having to speak
through an interpreter was a new experience. At that time
Nigeria was a British protectorate, and English was the
official language. However, each of some 250 tribes had
its own language. We were in the area of the Ibo people,
one of the most numerous groups, and the services were
in English and Ibo.

The church was in what had once been a large ware-
house. We had erected a large sign and outdoor lights,
which attracted many people. My subject that night was
"Jesus Christ the same yesterday, today, and forever." I
told them about Jesus being a Savior, the Healer of sick
bodies, and the Baptizer in the Holy Spirit, not only of
people in days gone by, but of all who put their faith in
Him today.

After the message, several came forward to pray for
salvation. Two young men, in beautiful, snow-white suits
— one leading the other — walked down the aisle,
greeted me, and introduced themselves. Reuben Okeiyi
had to be led because he was almost blind. Both were
school teachers, with good positions. But Reuben's sight
was failing. Now he faced the possibility of losing both
his eyesight and his vocation.

Reuben's condition was common in those days. It was

caused by eating improperly washed cassava. This is a root vegetable (like a long, thin potato) from which we get tapioca. The skin contains a deadly poison. After being peeled the cassava must be washed and soaked to remove all trace of the poison. If not, this will affect the eyes of those who eat it.

Women pounding cassava

As a poor student, Reuben had eaten the cheapest food possible — fufu, made from pounded cassava. Evidently some of it had not been prepared properly, and now he was going blind.

Reuben told me of his condition and reminded me of what I had said about Jesus healing people today. "Sir, is this true?" he asked. "Never have I heard of this before. I am a member of a church and attend regularly. We read about Jesus healing blind people, but it is always put back to the days when Jesus was on earth. Never have I heard that Jesus would heal a blind man today."

Repeating my text, I explained that Jesus had not changed. The things He did, He still does today, saving men from their sins and healing sick bodies.

"Sir, what shall I do?" Reuben asked.

I replied, "Reuben, there is only one thing for you to do. We will kneel here and pray together and ask God to come into your life in a new way. Then we will pray that He will touch your eyes and make you well again." The pastor and I explained the way of salvation, prayed with the young men, anointed Reuben with oil and prayed for his eyes.

Seemingly nothing happened that night, but the next evening Reuben was in the service and all smiles. He was happy because he knew God had forgiven his sins. He felt different and his eyes were better. The next week he attended every service and each night was seeing better until he was completely healed. Soon he received the baptism in the Holy Spirit.

When we started our Bible school in Umuahia, Reuben was one of the students and associate pastor there. He also helped with special teaching for those students with little education. Later he became a full-time teacher in the Bible school. He was a faithful, astute student of the Word of God.

As the years passed Reuben Okeiyi became one of the truly great preachers in Nigeria. His people called him the weeping prophet, because whenever the Holy Spirit especially moved upon Him as he ministered, tears would roll down his face.

For 17 years Reuben taught in the Nigerian Bible school until the Lord suddenly took him home. My first convert taught many of the older ministers who are still active today.

Getting Acquainted

As newly arrived missionaries, Dorothy and I soon noticed one outstanding characteristic of the Africans — their unfailing politeness. When people met they followed a familiar pattern in their greetings, inquiring about the wife, son, house, possessions, mother, and father. They were sincerely interested in all that concerned one another and us. These greetings sometimes lasted two or three minutes. I learned to follow this custom. If any family member was sick at home, we always stopped to pray for him. I learned from the people a lasting lesson in kindness and thoughtfulness.

There in Port Harcourt we began to get acquainted with the pastor and the people and to find our niche in the church services. When the people prayed, they all prayed together fervently and only stopped when the pastor rang a little bell. God has given the Africans a marvelous sense of rhythm and music. They sang choruses many times over with enthusiasm, while vigorously clapping their hands in a beautiful rhythmic pattern. Some clapped in one cadence and others in a different beat. Put together, it became beautiful, harmonious music. Some of the choruses were in Ibo, some in English. Some they had composed; others were translated from English.

One of my earliest impressions of our services among the small groups of churches in Iboland was their action whenever they sang the word "Jesus," "Lord," or "God." When they came to one of these words in a song, the men and boys automatically bowed, and the women and girls all curtsied. One of their early leaders had taught them to honor these names above every other name in the world.

There was joyous fervency but no excesses. If anyone got out of order, the pastor was quick to ring the bell and change the order of the service. They also had times of quiet worship and reverent singing of hymns. We sang these out of the hymnals of the Church of England until a number of years later the brethren at our printing press published our own songbooks in the vernacular and in English.

We soon observed other things about their customs and culture. In conversation it wasn't courteous to go directly to the main subject or problem to be dealt with. Long palaver about other things usually preceded the roundabout approach to the main purpose of the conversation.

There were special ways of doing things. I am left-handed, but learned from experience never to reach out my left hand to anyone or to take something from a person. That was a terrible insult. Many ways of doing things seemed strange to us at first, but as time went by we learned to adjust to them and fit in among the people where God had placed us.

Our African brethren became our friends in the truest sense of the word. At first they were a little uncomfortable in our home, for their experience had not always been very pleasant with white people. They would not sit down until urged to do so, and then sat on the edge of their chairs. Finally the day came when they could relax in our home.

Generally speaking, they did not like direct questions asked of them, nor would they ask them of others. However, as we got better acquainted, those reservations broke down. They would inquire, "Why would you let us into your house when other white people would not allow it?" My being lefthanded led to questions like, "Didn't your father teach you that it was wrong to be lefthanded?"

It was the custom for a man to eat alone, served by his wife. When he had finished, his wife and children ate. They asked me, "Why do you eat with your wife and son at the table with you?"

Then there were questions such as, "Are all Americans as tall as you? Do all Americans speak such strange English?" (They were used to British English with a different accent, and to pidgin English.)

They would bring visiting pastor friends to our house in Port Harcourt. After the greetings were over, the local pastor would say, "Now, Brother Phillips, tell them about the river that gets so hard in your country that you can walk on it." Of all the stories I told them, they were most interested in those about the snow and ice — frozen rivers. It was hard for them to believe that we could actually see our breath in winter, for their coldest weather was not below 60 degrees Fahrenheit (15 degrees Celsius).

There is a special joy in fellowshiping with people of another culture, especially if you have had a part in bringing them the gospel. It was a thrill to see them grow in the knowledge of God, deeply gratifying and humbling as well.

Taking Communion

Always when I take communion my mind goes back to the Lord's Supper in Africa. At that time there was no grape juice available. And the pastor didn't want his members to drink wine, even if it was diluted. He consulted Dorothy about what to do. She suggested boiling sugar cane juice until it darkened, then diluting it with water. This type of "wine" became common in all our churches until grape juice was available. And I think God understood and approved!

More important was the preparation of the heart. In the early days, special services on Friday and Saturday were held for this purpose before the monthly communion service on Sunday. The pastor taught that the Lord's Supper was a sacred occasion, not to be entered into with anything in their hearts not pleasing to God, or anything against a brother.

One communion Sunday our pastor preached on the need of heart preparation. He had a beautiful white bath towel which, he emphasized, was what our hearts should look like in the sight of God. Then he preached a fine sermon. At its conclusion, he called two of the deacons to bring a basin of water and some soap. Then he asked them, "Did you wash your hands this morning?"

They both assured him they had.

The pastor replied, "So did I. Now I want you to wet your hands in the water, lather them with the soap but don't rinse them. Then dry them on this white towel." I knew that the deacons and congregation were puzzled, but they followed the pastor's directions.

When the pastor held up what had been a snow-white towel, it was now dirty where each man had wiped his hands. Then the pastor pointed out that in our casual life, touching our furniture and other items in our homes, our hands are soiled. "Just so, our hearts are made dirty by our contact with a sinful world," he said. "Without knowing it we become dirty and need the cleansingof the blood of Christ."

Learning About the Beginnings

When Dorothy and I arrived in Nigeria in 1940 there were already 11 Assemblies of God churches that had been organized by Lloyd Shirer the previous year. Naturally we were anxious to learn about the great revival in which they began. Lloyd told us about it. Later we found more details in *The History of the Assemblies of God in Nigeria* by George Alioha, one of the first baptized in the Holy Spirit among the Ibos.

In 1930 Augustus E. Wogu, from the Old Umuahia community (a section of the Umuahia township), was converted in Port Harcourt where he was working. He joined the Faith Tabernacle Church, a fundamental group. As Augustus went daily from house to house preaching and sharing the gospel, word reached his relatives that he had lost his mind.

In January 1931 Augustus Wogu went home for a weekend. His family saw that he was not crazy but had a sound mind. As he preached, a young man, George Alioha, accepted Christ. From that day on, George preached Jesus to all, especially to his friends.

Persecution followed as George Alioha preached in the area of Umuahia in 1931. Converts were driven from their homes. Their clothing and possessions were seized. Husbands opposed wives. One pastor was imprisoned for preaching in the village square and breaking the power of the jujus or fetishes.

But the Lord began to bring together people who experienced a spiritual awakening. When asked what denomination they belonged to, they replied that they belonged to Jesus. Later they called themselves the Church of Jesus Christ.

As there was no Faith Tabernacle Church in Old Umuahia, the people attended a church three miles away in Umuahia. God used these young people to bring a mighty revival to Faith Tabernacle. They were certain the second coming of the Lord was at hand.

Although there was no teaching about the baptism in the Holy Spirit, these believers searched the Word, desiring to worship God just as the New Testament believers had done. Providentially they found and read a copy of the *Pentecostal Evangel*. They now had the address of the Gospel Publishing House and wrote for books and other materials. These, and materials from other sources helped them greatly.

As they read the Word, studied and followed the Bible teaching, they were convinced that the baptism in the Holy Spirit was for them today. So in August, 1934, Augustus Wogu asked the leaders of Faith Tabernacle for teaching on this experience.

However, the leaders refused to accept that the baptism given on the Day of Pentecost was for the church today and did not want members who held such a doctrine. So the believers from Old Umuahia, courteously told the leaders that they were leaving.

Back in Old Umuahia, they fasted, prayed, and confessed their sins. Not one had ever seen anyone receive the baptism in the Holy Spirit, but they believed God's promise. They had a "house of prayer," and August Asonye became their first pastor.

August was visiting in Port Harcourt in 1934, when the first persons were baptized in the Holy Spirit. Mark Asonye, August's younger brother, was the first to receive this experience. Many others were filled with the Spirit at that time. Among them were August Asonye and Joseph Anyafulu.

Pastor August Asonye with student pastors of four churches that his church mothered

They returned to Old Umuahia full of the Holy Spirit. The church members there, like the household of Cornelius, were hungry, ready, and waiting when August and Joseph told them what God had done. Before the sermon could even be preached, God filled many with His Holy Spirit with the evidence of speaking in other tongues. A revival began! This outpouring increased as the believers continued to pray, consecrate themselves, and testify, for everyone became a preacher, spreading the good news.

After separating from the Faith Tabernacle organization, the Church of Jesus Christ sought affiliation with some missionary organization from which they could receive teaching, helps, and training for their pastors. Again they fasted and prayed for help. God gave them visions of missionaries coming by airplanes and ships and unloading their luggage. So, they wrote to various groups in the United States, Great Britain, and South Africa, telling of their doctrines and asking for missionaries.

They acted in faith and built a large house for the missionaries that God would send them. For three years they kept it clean and empty — waiting for God's answer to their prayers.

Meanwhile, unknown to the believers in Iboland, God had poured out His Spirit on some Christians of the Annang and Ibibio tribes in the district of Calabar, east of Port Harcourt. Their work had spread even more rapidly than among the Ibos. They too wanted help and wrote to the Foreign Missions Department of the Assemblies of God asking for missionaries.

So, the Missions Committee had two appeals for help from two different Pentecostal groups in Nigeria, neither one knowing that the other existed. They considered these requests, together with the appeal to Brother Flower and Brother Perkin at the Lagos airport, and decided to send someone to survey the field and give his recommendation

At their request, missionary Lloyd Shirer went from the West African country of the Gold Coast (now Ghana) to Port Harcourt in June 1939. He spent some time visiting the churches in both Calabar and Iboland, then recommended approval for their affiliation with the Assemblies of God.

On a second trip, this time with his wife, he stayed longer. In September, 1939, they met in Port Harcourt with the pastors and executives of the Church of Jesus Christ. After agreeing on doctrine, practice, and church government, they drew up and adopted a constitution and by-laws and formed the Iboland District Council of the Assemblies of God. W. Lloyd Shirer became the District Superintendent, with George M. Alioha as the Assistant District Superintendent.

In the same way, the Pentecostal leaders in Calabar met with the Shirers in their church at Ikot Ekpene and organized the Annang and Ibibio District Council of the Assemblies of God Mission. Lloyd Shirer would serve as the District Superintendent, and Udom Akpan as the Assistant District Superintendent.

At the same time Dorothy and I were finalizing our preparations to go to Nigeria. The Shirers told the churches that we were coming and made plans for establishing a Bible school for training the pastors as soon as we could do so. They would stay with us some months to help in this and other work.

How thrilled we were when we arrived in February, 1940, to hear of the growth in both groups during the four or five years of their existence! There were some 50 churches scattered through the district of Calabar, and 15 congregations in Iboland.

We thought we would live in Calabar, to minister to the majority of the churches, and reach out to Iboland, too. But God had other plans for us.

CHAPTER THREE

Tragedy and Triumph

Problems in Calabar Province

The Shirers had spent several months ministering among the Calabar churches. Several years had passed since the beginning of the great revival there — all this time without any missionary supervision or Bible training for the pastors. A strong national leader, Udom Akpan, had taken control of the churches and pastors. He and the pastors were now far from the spirituality of the early revival. They seemed interested only in increasing the number of members without regard to their spiritual condition. Large memberships meant large incomes for the pastors!

Many of the "converts" were still deeply involved in heathen practices and had brought some of them into the churches as part of their worship. Some would eat pages of the Bible, sacrifice chickens and spread their blood on the altar for forgiveness of sins.

How they needed teaching! The Ibo believers had been greatly helped by studying the Bible, the *Pentecostal Evangel,* and other teaching materials. How different it was in Calabar where the people depended totally on their leaders!

Facing the Issue

When Lloyd Shirer visited them, he found that the leaders rejected the idea of a Bible school. He advised us that unless their attitude changed it would be better to give up the work there and concentrate on work in the Ibo tribe. However, before doing this, Lloyd and I decided to visit Calabar together and see if the Lord would change their attitude.

Lloyd sent telegrams to the church leaders in Calabar, asking them to meet us in Ikot Ekpene, one of the large towns of the province. There we met with pastor Udom Akpan in his church, along with about 50 pastors and several hundred people. They spent about an hour greeting me as the new missionary, and presented me with many gifts: dozens and dozens of eggs, yams, bananas, cassava, and even a live goat.

Brother Shirer called the meeting to order and announced the first order of business: a Bible school for training pastors. He asked them to speak to that subject. But in the customary manner they spoke about everything else first — their churches, how greatly they had grown, their experience of salvation and divine healing, and on and on. They mentioned the idea of a Bible school, but only as a sort of side issue.

After several hours of this, I finally asked some specific questions. Still they continued to answer in long stories. At last I asked directly: "Will you, Brother Udom, attend Bible school when it is open?"

When I insisted on an answer, he said: "No." He could not, it would be "belittling to him." He was an "honored pastor" among his people. For him to go to school would be "insulting."

One by one I asked the other pastors if they would attend Bible school. After long hesitations and strange, mixed-up answers, they all said they would not attend Bible school.

I then questioned them to find out if they would encourage their young people to attend Bible school. After a long discussion about it, Brother Udom said that they would permit a limited number of their young men to attend Bible school, but they would have to have a deciding voice in what was taught and about any changes in teaching that we might introduce.

To my great sorrow we faced an impossible situation. These pastors desperately needed Bible teaching but were too proud to admit it. Also, they knew that if their young men attended Bible school, a clash would come between the graduates and the untrained pastors.

Lloyd and I returned with heavy hearts to the government rest house where we were staying. We prayed until late that night. Over and over Lloyd prayed: "If only a Bible teacher had come to Calabar ten years ago, even before the Holy Spirit was outpoured, the people would have received the truth and shunned the heathen practices they have brought into the church."

Teaching the Word! Teaching the Word would have saved thousands of hungry, untaught people. A great revival and no teacher of the Word! Why? Oh why?

The next morning we met with 40 of the leading Calabar pastors. I gave them my decision: "Since you brothers refuse to be taught in Bible school, there is nothing I can do for you. Goodbye, and God bless you." What a tragedy! After one day's discussion I had severed all connection with Calabar. The decision of the pastors there seemed irrevocable.

It could have all been so different. Years later I met a minister and his wife in America whom God had definitely called to Calabar. He gave them each that name when neither knew that such a place existed. He was a wonderful teacher. That was at about the time that the great revival began in Calabar. They were willing to go, but let friends dissuade them and never answered God's call. How they wept when they learned the tragic results of their disobedience!

Contrast in Umuahia

Before returning to Port Harcourt from Ikot Ekpene, Lloyd and I visited Old Umuahia and had a conference with the local pastor and some of his leading men. What a difference in attitude! We had planned to have a Bible school in Ikot Ekpene, but God had planned for it to be in Old Umuahia. On this visit we saw the house that by faith the people had built for our home! Some months later we would move there.

Anguished Prayer and Eventual Answer

When we got back to Port Harcourt, Lloyd and I told our wives about the meeting in Ikot Ekpene. That night Dorothy and I prayed and wept in anguish of spirit. After all the years of preparation, hopes, and prayers, we were in Nigeria. Yet in just one week's time, all our dreams about Calabar had been smashed. However, some day God would answer those anguished prayers, and there would be Assemblies of God churches scattered all over Calabar Province. But there would be much hard work and prayer before that time.

Guidance Even in Disappointment

The disappointment of having to turn away from Calabar lingered for a long time. Had I made a mistake, giving up that area in one day's quick decision? Dorothy and I were unhappy about giving up the large work in Calabar and accepting the oversight of the relatively tiny group of people in Iboland.

Then God gave me this Scripture: "Behold, I will proceed to do a marvelous work among this people, even a marvelous work and a wonder" (Isaiah 29:14). At first I had difficulty in believing it, for I saw no signs of anything great in Iboland. However, in the following days God made this promise very real to me.

Short-Term Bible School

Following our Calabar experience, Lloyd suggested that he and I arrange for a one-month) Bible training course in Old Umuahia. Dorothy and I couldn't understand why she and Margaret couldn't go too. But the Shirers understood that if they went and took Donald, the only white child the people had ever seen, very little study would be accomplished. In addition to the students, people would come by the hundreds from all around to see this unbelievable white child.

Dorothy and Margaret had taken Don to the market with them one evening. When they walked into the market, people crowded around and were trampling on one another to get close enough to see Don. Tables and chairs were knocked over. Farm produce lay scattered everywhere. Some of the men from our church, seeing the situation, came to the rescue and hurried Don and the two women home.

Having Don in a church service created a problem at that time, for all eyes were on him from beginning to end. Everything he did or said was interesting. After the service the people wanted to touch him.

So, just Lloyd and I drove to Old Umuahia. We had a most profitable month of Bible school with the pastors of Iboland. Some had walked more than 25 miles (40 kilometers) to attend. Others came on bicycles, and still others by train. With shouts of greetings, broad smiles, and hugs of affection, they met as friends in joyful expectation of an answer to their prayers for years.

The local church became the chapel, classroom, and dormitory; and the pastor's house was the dining room. Using the church benches for seats and unplaned planks on boxes for desks, in cramped conditions, the pastors studied and never complained.

We made copies of the studies on a Multigraph machine

for classes in The Doctrine of God, Typology, The Pastor and His Work, Personal Evangelism, and Bible. Lloyd and I taught two classes each morning and one in the afternoon.

Sometimes the power of God would fall, so studies were laid aside while the Holy Spirit dealt with hearts. The teachers were refreshed by the novel way the students expressed themselves in examinations, their keen insight into some phases of the work, and — most of all — by their insatiable hunger for the Word.

As the culminating activity of the month's studies, the students told what God had done for them. They spoke of the joy in their hearts and of thankfulness to God for the privilege of attending this school. Then Lloyd and I handed out fellowship certificates to the 14 workers who had qualified. On the next day the pastors returned to their churches with a greater knowledge of God's Word and a deeper sense of their responsibility.

Pastors in first term of Bible school, 1940

Left on Our Own

Before the Shirers left they took Dorothy, Don, and me to visit all of the Assemblies of God churches in Iboland, introducing us to the people. They had been a real guide to us and to the Ibo churches. I would have the responsibility of overseeing these churches as Superintendent after the Shirers left.

Early one morning, after helping us for six months, Lloyd and Margaret packed their car for the long journey back to the Gold Coast. After praying together, Dorothy, Don, and I waved goodbye to them and watched their car as long as we could see it. We were alone! Now we were in Africa on our own. In all of our previous years we had always had someone to go to for advice and counsel. But now, in a foreign country and working with people of another culture, we had to depend on God in a new way. Psalm 73:24 took on a new meaning: "Thou shalt guide me with thy counsel and afterward receive me to glory."

A few months later we moved from Port Harcourt to Old Umuahia. This would be the location of the Bible school and a better center for work among the Ibos.

Reinforcements!

The work was growing among the Ibos. Both churches and members were being "added daily" to the Assemblies of God, and we needed more missionaries. The Department of Foreign Missions was aware of our need for additional help, and prospective missionaries were applying for visas for Nigeria. However, because of the war in Europe, travel was greatly restricted.

To our delight one day in April, 1941, we received a cable saying, "Enroute to Nigeria, Rex Jackson." Days passed while we waited. Finally another telegram came from Lagos, the capital and main port city of Nigeria. Rex had arrived there and would reach Port Harcourt by train in three days. Imagine our joy! At last God was sending us another missionary. We didn't know if he was single or married.

Those three days passed slowly. Then a crowd of excited church members and two happy missionaries met at the train station. Out of the train stepped a tall young man, all smiles, to be greeted by many people. How can I describe the happy days that followed? Pastors and church members came all the rest of that day and the next to meet the new missionary.

Rex had been near the end of his senior year at Great Lakes Bible Institute in Zion, Illinois, when he received a telegram from the Missions Department asking if he could leave the next week for Nigeria. He had applied for missionary appointment to Nigeria the previous summer, but had been turned down because he was not married. Then war conditions got so bad that captains of ships crossing the Atlantic refused to take women and children because of the danger from German submarines. With that, no married couples could go, but one captain had said he would take single men.

Now Rex had to apply for a passport, secure a visa, get to New York, and buy his equipment — in a week. Fortunately the ship was delayed a week or he would never have made it. When the ship sailed, Rex was on it headed for West Africa! Although he was not able to complete his classwork at Great Lakes, the Bible school graduated him with honors.

We soon saw Rex's deep dedication to the work of God. Shortly after his arrival, news came from Calabar that the leader of the work in that area, Udom Akpan, had died. One pastor was appealing again to the Assemblies of God for help. Rex and I talked about the need and agreed that Calabar should be given another chance for the sake of the thousands of people involved. Rex felt that God was leading him there.

Meanwhile, the work among the Ibos was growing so rapidly that we were again in desperate need of help. One day in late 1941, while busy at the Bible school, we received a telegram, "Have arrived. Am at the port in Port Harcourt. Elmer Frink."

We had never heard of Elmer Frink. God had called him to Nigeria while he was a student at Central Bible College. Soon after graduation he received missionary appointment and was on his way. In two hours after receiving his telegram we were in Port Harcourt to meet him, and that evening were back on the Bible school hill with the new missionary. Rex arrived the next day to meet the newcomer. What a happy time of fellowship! Our cups were full to overflowing!

In the rest of the 1940's 30 more missionaries responded to God's call to Nigeria. They strengthened the work, expanded the training program, and helped open new fields to the gospel. (See Appendix.)

The Phillips family, Elmer Frink, and Rex Jackson

*Rex
and
Martha
Jackson.*

Elmer had brought a Chevrolet panel truck, so he and Rex agreed to use it by turn, month by month, as they would be in different areas. They would use bicycles the rest of the time.

We spent many days and evenings with Rex and Elmer discussing the future of the work. Each made his own decision, with the approval of all, as to what he felt God was leading him to do. Dorothy and I would stay at the Bible school. Elmer would supervise the Ovoro area of Iboland, where we had new churches and the possibility of many more. And Rex, after several visits into Calabar Province, moved there.

Both men helped in the Bible school program as their time permitted. They were wonderful additions to our staff. In one way we were a marvel to the students. Ibo people are short. I am 6 feet and 2 inches tall; Rex and Elmer were both taller than I! Our Nigerian Christians were proud of us and said, "They are our big people," which could also mean "people of great importance."

Elmer married Betty Hall who had come to Nigeria in 1944. In 1948 Betty, like many early missionaries, died of blackwater fever. Elmer returned to the States and worked from then on with the Elim Mission.

Slow Growth in Calabar

After three years in Ikot Ekpene, Rex went back to the United States and married Martha Safford, a dedicated minister and teacher in the Great Lakes Bible Institute. He came back to Calabar Province with his bride and they worked there for two more years.

Rex had gone to Calabar with the hope of pulling together some of the churches — or at least some of the people who wanted to do God's will. Some of the new missionaries were also stationed in that area for a while. But time after time there were disappointments. The pastor who had asked for help was not faithful to the Lord.

None of the original churches came back into the Assemblies. However, the Word was being sown among other people where it would eventually bear fruit.

The missionaries left and went to other areas. But God chose a young man from Calabar working in Iboland and converted there as His instrument for a new revival. His wife was an Ibo who helped him in many respects. He studied the Word in Bible school and felt led to go back to his people. God blessed his ministry. As he and missionaries who reentered that region taught the Word, strong churches were built on its solid foundation. Now there are about 100 Assemblies of God churches all over Calabar Province and a Bible school where new workers are trained!

Missionaries in 1970

CHAPTER FOUR

Trails and New Churches

On Trek Visiting the Churches

A good part of our work involved visiting the churches and preaching in the unevangelized towns and villages on the way. Wherever we traveled, we put in our car everything we would need, depending on where we were going. Always there was an extra can of gas, some food, and filtered water. If we were staying overnight, we carried camp cots, bedding, mosquito nets, cooking pots, and other things.

Always one of our household workers (generally called "houseboys" then) accompanied me when I went on an overnight trip. First of all, they were Christians and ready to give their testimony. They helped me with the problems of understanding the culture of the people, as they knew about the heathen customs.

We had a permanent arrangement when we went "on trek" that the Lord's work came first. I told them that the Lord's work was theirs as well as mine. What a joy it was to hear them on their own explaining what the Christian life was all about, and telling new converts what to do with their jujus and idols.

More and more I realized how ignorant I was of these people's lives, their culture, their heathen background, and how deep the changes were when they became new creatures in Christ Jesus.

When I visited the different churches, the church platform became my bedroom, living room, and dining room, as the people didn't have guest rooms or a room in their homes big enough for me and my camping equipment. Richard, our cook, took charge. With the help of many willing hands, everything was supplied. My car was emptied, my camp cot set up on the platform, a folding table put up, and water brought for my water filter. A stalk of bananas was tied to the ceiling, while people brought oranges, eggs, chickens, and everything you could think of to eat as gifts for the visiting missionary.

By this time the people were in church, so we began a service. In due time, the elders of the town arrived. Everything stopped while they were greeted in a special way. Finally, at the urging of the pastor, the people were dismissed so that I could have tea and get ready for the evening service.

The custom in all of our churches was to have two services a day, one at five o'clock in the morning and the other at five o'clock in the evening. These services were a wonderful time of singing and praying. One after another led in prayer about what they felt was important: the persecution that was common in those days, the crops, the weather, their village and its chief, the salvation of their heathen family members, the sick among them. Each service ended with a short exhortation from the Word.

The people needed to get home before dark, so, after they left I had time to relax and reflect on what God was doing for them, while Richard heated water over a fire outside for a pot of tea. He killed a chicken, dressed and fried it in a short time. With the fruit and meat I had a big meal. I wasn't used to such service, but it was the custom in Africa.

Having read many books on how to be a good missionary, I determined I was going to eat with the Africans. They told me in our first Bible school session that I couldn't eat their food, because all white men told them it was too hot with pepper. I tried but found that their gravy was so hot with red pepper that it was impossible for me to eat it. They said, "Brother Phillips, we will make you food without the pepper and then you can eat it." This they did. And when I was on trek, the people gave us food, but our cook prepared it — without the hot peppers!

One day Richard suggested making bread since he had some flour in the "chop box" (food box). He had no yeast or baking powder, but to my amazement used a little palm wine as leavening to make it rise. He then took an empty 5-gallon can in which we had bought kerosene or gasoline, and with a knife and hammer cut around three sides of one end, to make the oven door. He then dug a hole in the ground, lay the can on its side in the hole, and half-buried it, piling dirt around the sides. Next he built a fire around the outside of his "stove." After the dough had risen, he put it in a tin and put it into the oven, keeping the fire going around the outside of the can.

That evening I had hot baked bread and honey! Honey was always available. The people would raid a tree where the bees had made their hive, even though the bees stung them, and would get a gallon or two of honey, which they sold. But you couldn't find bread like this for many miles in any direction. Some honey on my hot bread was wonderful (even if it did have a faint odor of palm wine), especially when we were at least 500 miles (800 kilometers) from a store!

After supper I could lean back in my folding canvas chair and watch for falling stars. Nigerian nights were not like those we were used to in the States. Star formations are different in the Southern Hemisphere, much brighter. Night sounds were different too — no traffic sounds or loud noises — only the quiet murmur of voices from the pastor's compound.

As daylight faded, I began to hear the tentative sound of drums — some near, some far away — beginning their nightly serenade. First was the highpitched voice of the boys' drums, which are no larger than my two hands. Then came the deep-throated grumble of the village drums, some more than six-feet long, cut from a large tree and hollowed out by careful burning and chipping with primitive tools.

These large drums talk together from miles away. Each drummer, trained from childhood, has an individual "fist" that the African listeners easily recognized. But I was unable to understand the various changes in rhythm, the variation in tone, the long pauses while the drummer waited for a reply. Sleep came slowly with this beautiful, night-long serenade.

Carrying Loads

Traveling on the roads in Nigeria was always an interesting experience. People on foot carried everything on their heads-from a box of matches to heavy loads of cloth, yams, cassava, or stacks of wood. It was not unusual to see a 70- or 80-pound girl carrying a load on her head, a log I couldn't lift from the ground. Several men or women would lift a log from the ground, and a girl would walk under it and move around a bit until it was correctly balanced on her head. Then she would walk off carrying it home to be split for firewood. She might have to carry it as far as five miles (eight kilometers). It wasn't hard for her to do, for she had been carrying something on her head since the day she could walk.

Sometimes I took Dorothy with me to visit the churches. If a church knew we were coming, crowds were often waiting for us, even though they didn't know the exact time of our arrival. Drums always sent the message out through the village. In no time at all, people came running from every direction.

It was easy to unload the car, for everyone helped. When I took out my briefcase to carry it, someone would take it so that I had nothing in my hands. I didn't notice that Dorothy was coming behind me loaded down with things in both hands and under her arms. This happened twice, then Dorothy called it to my attention. So, I told her that at the next church we visited we would teach the people a lesson.

At the next church, the people came running as always. They emptied my hands of everything and left Dorothy to carry her load. Then I turned to Dorothy, took the load from her hands, and started toward the church. There was a sudden cessation of all activity. Then two men came to me hesitantly and said, "Sir, we will carry these things too." And so they took from my hands the things that Dorothy had been carrying.

That day I violated a national custom. Women were the carriers. It was strange for them to see me carry a woman's load. They said: "That's the way these white people behave as far as their wives are concerned."

Richard told us that the people believed the missionary's wife was weak. She couldn't carry loads very well, so her husband, being stronger, carried her loads. Richard laughed as he said to us: "If they could see Madam when she has to move the furniture around the house, they wouldn't think she was weak!"

"Are You the Man With the Book?"

I usually traveled to visit the churches every other month or so. However, I visited some of the older churches only once in six or seven months, as I knew they were carrying on well enough.

As more and more churches were started, some of which had only part-time pastors, I would visit and teach them many things needed by new congregations.

I always took care to talk with the older men. They told me about a man called "Prophet Harris." The Encyclopedia Britannica (British edition) reports that Prophet Harris came from Liberia to Nigeria before missionaries arrived in this country. He had a revelation from God. Using a New Testament, he preached separation from heathenism. Like an Old Testament prophet, he said: "Separate yourselves from sin. There is a man coming with a Book one day who will tell you how you can be free from your sins."

The first time I heard his name was when I was deep in the interior of Nigeria. An old man asked me in broken English if I was the man Prophet Harris said would come with a book. I replied, "I don't know this Prophet Harris. Who was he?"

"He was a great African who came. Our grandfathers told us about him and of the great things he said. He promised us that a white man would come with a Book one day to show us the way out of our heathen sins and evil practices."

After being asked that same question by older people in several towns, I realized there must be something to the story I was hearing. And since I always had a Bible with me, I would tell them, "Yes, I'm the man. I'm the very man that Prophet Harris talked to your grandfathers about. Would you like me to read some of the book?" And I read to them, sometimes by the hour, especially to the older people whose grandfathers had told them about Prophet Harris.

I always began in Genesis with the creation of Adam and Eve, how they fell into sin, and how God provided a sacrifice for them and for mankind. I explained that God for a time made provision for sin with the blood of animals or birds. Later He sent His Son to do away with all other sacrifices. Ah, they would listen to this! Then I would ask, "What do you do about the sins of your family?"

"Oh, we save money for a goat or sheep, or even a cow, and once a year we make a sacrifice."

"How many years have you done this?" I asked.

Shaking their heads they said, "We have always done this, and our fathers and their fathers before us. It is all we know."

"1Has it taken away your sins?"

With much indignation they answered, "Our young people are worse now than we are. They don't know what they're doing; they live in sin."

While I don't know what all the results have been in those areas, I know that God sent a prophet with a message like that of John the Baptist to prepare the hearts of the people for me and for others who would bring "the Book." Today in many of those towns we have thriving Assemblies of God churches.

Left: Student leaving Bible school for a pastorate Right: Giving out tracts and inviting to Sunday school

CHAPTER FIVE

Dorothy's Work in Nigeria

Vision Fulfilled in Port Harcourt

Although Dorothy seldom spoke of it, I knew she had not forgotten the vision God had given her as a highschool girl. Only a kilometer (about half a mile) from our house in Port Harcourt was the Bonny River, a part of the great Niger River which she had seen in her vision. God had shown her then that she would be working with the women.

The women in the Port Harcourt church were delighted to have a missionary wife meet with them almost every week. It was love at first sight. A white woman was an unusual sight in those days. Dorothy would sit and talk with them about their homes, their families, and their experiences with the Lord.

Dorothy Phillips and Stella Ezeigbo

A few weeks after we were settled, Dorothy suggested having the women meet together once a week. They met in the church and arranged a program. The women spoke "pidgin English" but they wanted to learn proper English. Only a few could read their Ibo language. Dorothy couldn't help them in that, but because of her urging, pastors were encouraged to teach the women to read Ibo. Although they had little if any schooling, they possessed marvelous memories and memorized long portions of Scripture.

In addition to Bible studies in these meetings they learned practical skills. They didn't know how to sew, knit, or crochet. So they enthusiastically approved learning these skills.

After we moved to Umuahia, the women's work became Dorothy's interest in all of our churches. Many times the teaching seemed hopelessly slow, for their customs went back for generations. Most came from a heathen background in which everything people did related in some way to a heathen custom or god. The tools they used, everything in the house, every member of the family, every birth, every death — all were directly related to some pagan deity. But little by little they learned and followed God's way. These women became a strong spiritual force in all phases of the work in our churches.

Teaching Child Care

In 1940, the year we arrived, the Nigerian government stated that of all recorded births in that country, at least 50% of the babies died before they were a year old. We saw that one reason was that they weren't kept dry and warm.

In the sewing hour for the women in the Port Harcourt church, Dorothy taught them how to knit and sew for their families. One young woman knit an outfit for her baby which was due in a month. She then went back to her hometown for its birth.

One wet, chilly day she came to show us her newborn child. Taking it from the carrying cloth on her back, she proudly displayed the three-day-old infant. Its small, naked body was glistening with rain. Dorothy brought the mother and child into the house where is was warmer. She asked, "Where is the garment you knit for your baby? It is cold, and the baby can't stand this weather."

"Oh," replied the mother, "that's for when I take the baby to church. I'm saving it till next Sunday."

Dorothy found some cloth and wrapped the baby in it. When the mother left, she had strict instructions on how to keep the baby warm and dry.

On another chilly, rainy day Dorothy and I overtook a member of one of our churches on the road, so we stopped to give her a ride. She had a headload of things she was going to sell in the market, and was carrying her newborn baby on her back.

When a baby is strapped tightly to its mother's back, its head is invariably turned sideways between the mother's shoulder blades with its face looking up. As soon as the mother got into the car she unwrapped the baby from her back and began to dry its skin, only to discover the baby was dead. It had literally drowned! The rain pouring down over the shoulders of the mother had run into the mouth and nose of that newborn infant, causing its death.

Dorothy soon met opposition to her teaching about nutrition, health, and hygiene. She taught the women to boil their drinking water and to give their babies orange juice. But when the younger women went home the older women scoffed at such things.

She learned about a practice in childbirth that caused many deaths. One bright and beautiful young student, the wife of a pastor, was expecting a child. Dorothy helped her prepare for its coming. However, the family followed the usual custom for its birth. Babies were to be born in the yard, not in the house. And most of the time the yards were muddy because of the extremely heavy rainfall. At the time of delivery the mothers were placed on the ground. If the baby was slow in being born, the grandma, wishing to help in the best way she knew, would jump on her daughter's stomach to assist in the child's birth. This is what happened to the lovely and consecrated young pastor's wife. She died in the ordeal. You can see why Dorothy was determined to teach the women some better ways than the ones they knew then!

A Daily Clinic

Dorothy had been in nurse's training and already had some experience in this work at the time we were married. So she started ministering to the sick soon after we arrived in Africa. We arose early every morning to meet an unbelievable variety of needs: sick babies — some with worms, some injured, one who had fallen into the fire. Boils, carbuncles, and cuts that needed cleaning and sewing up.

Guinea worms were problem. These ugly things came from drinking impure water. The worms developed inside a person. When they reached a certain stage, they began burrowing out through a foot. They were long worms, and great care had to be taken in trying to remove them. You had to pull the worm out just a little way and wind it around a stick as you pulled. Then the stick and worm were bound to the ankle. If you were careful, you could get the whole worm out in a week's time. However, if you pulled too hard and broke it, the guinea worm would die and putrefy inside the foot, causing a very serious condition which might result in permanent lameness or worse.

Dorothy had obtained a great quantity of sulfa drugs in tablet form. She had the tablets pounded into powder and used this antibiotic for many needs.

Also, Dorothy trained a young man, Abel, to be her assistant. As they worked with each patient, Abel became a wonderful helper in dealing with the people, both physically and spiritually. If we had to be away, Abel was in charge and carried on faithfully.

Personal Health and Answered Prayer

We could never have accomplished what we did, or even been able to remain on the field, if it had not been for the prayers of others that sustained us. A never-ending list of daily activities began for Dorothy every morning but Sunday. Long before we got out of bed we would hear the quiet murmur of voices and sometimes the cry of a baby outside our house where people were waiting for her help. She had classes for women, taught in the Bible school, tutored students who couldn't speak or write English, kept the household running, took part in the church services, taught Don his school lessons, and sometimes went with me when I traveled to visit the churches. On occasion she would supervise the construction workers to keep them from slowing down on the job while I was gone, or she would drive the truck to Port Harcourt, 70 miles away, for supplies.

The constant activity caused Dorothy to lose weight. When we arrived in Africa she was quite plump, but in the first six months she lost 45 pounds without missing a meal. She was quite happy about losing the excess pounds, but our pastors sorrowed for her and for me in her loss of weight. They solemnly asked her about her health and she told them she felt wonderful. They would never mention her loss of weight — not to her! But they discussed it freely among themselves. In that area both men and women wanted to be stout. It was a sign of grace, a sign of the blessing of God. To have a fat wife was an honor for a man. Some of them came to me and said, "Sir, we are sorry for you. You had such a beautiful wife when you came to Nigeria. Now she is so thin. We feel you are being cheated."

Although Dorothy didn't seem to be ill otherwise, she began to suffer with severe headaches. We were not too concerned at first, for we assumed they would go away. Perhaps they were caused by the tropical sun. So every time we left the house Dorothy wore heavy, dark glasses, and pulled her sun helmet down over her forehead. We prayed daily about it, and our Nigerian churches faithfully prayed for her. But many months passed before there was a change.

We didn't write home about her need, for we didn't want her mother to know. We felt she had enough to bear; her family strongly opposed her Pentecostal faith and never missed an opportunity to say something about Dorothy's marrying a preacher. Now he had taken her and Don to die in Africa!

We continued praying — desperately. We asked that the Spirit would lead someone to pray for Dorothy, but 10 months went by without any answer. Then suddenly the headaches disappeared, never to return. Someone had touched God for us, and we were happy.

Years later a young woman in Alton, Illinois, Alvena Goring, asked Dorothy, "Mrs. Phillips, was there ever a time when you needed prayer, especially for your head? We prayed for you regularly, but one night I was awakened out of a sound sleep with a strong impression to pray for you. As I looked up into the darkness, I saw the top of your head, your eyes and forehead, and your blond hair. So I got out of bed on a cold winter night, covered myself with a blanket, and prayed earnestly until suddenly the burden went away. Were you ever in serious physical need?"

Dorothy explained about the headaches and why she didn't write about them. "Alvena, when you prayed my headaches went away, never to return!" God answered our prayers, using Alvena to intercede for us!

Taking Care of Don

Nigeria presented various problems for us as we were raising our son, Donald. We wanted him to have a good education, and Dorothy taught him the Calvert Correspondence School lessons. His grades were good, but how would he get along with other children?

Since Don was the only white child for a thousand miles around, people would defer to him in almost everything. Sometimes I assigned certain tasks to him and assumed that he did them. Then I happened to hear something not intended for my ears. Don was telling one of the boys to do the job I had told him to do. There was no complaint; the boy was happy to do what Don demanded! Of course we settled this with Don and his friend, but the basic problem remained: he was being spoiled and not learning to work.

Don was being raised among a people who loved him and would do almost anything for him. He learned their language early. While Dorothy and I were struggling as one of the men tried to teach us Ibo, Don was able to explain something I couldn't understand.

Adapting to African culture was easy for Don. He was in and out of the people's homes, eating their food, learning their customs, and beginning to think like they did. This was excellent preparation for his work as a missionary in later years, but he also needed to learn about his own country and its culture. We had been in Nigeria three years, the usual term of missionary service in malaria-infested West Africa before taking a furlough. Because of conditions during the Second World War, a furlough was not possible for at least another year. We decided to send Don ahead to relatives in America.

Dr. and Mrs. Will Carlson, Baptist missionaries and dear friends, were going home and agreed to take Don with them. They left Port Harcourt on a DC-3 — not considered a plane fit to fly over the ocean in those days. It was fitted with bucket seats along the side of the fuselage. At the feet of the passengers, fastened to the floor between the rows of seats, were large spare gas tanks. It was a long and dangerous flight, especially dangerous since some passengers insisted on smoking during the flight with those loaded gas tanks at their feet!

In Miami, Dr. Carlson put Don on another plane for Cleveland and sent a telegram to relatives. He also sent a telegram to a close friend of Dorothy's uncle. He was an advisor to the president in Washington D.C., where Don had to change planes. Fortunately he was able to help Don change planes and keep his place from being taken by a military officer who needed it. (During the war civilians had to give up seats if they were needed by the military.) And so, a lonesome eight-year-old boy from Africa, carrying an American flag, wearing a sun helmet, and with a kimono for an overcoat, arrived at the Cleveland airport to meet relatives whom he scarcely remembered.

Many years later, after Don and his wife, Theola, had served as missionaries in Africa and were teaching in the Bible school in Holland, he wrote us a letter about how those early years in Nigeria impressed him:

"Dear Dad and Mom,

In looking back over the years since going with you for the first time to Nigeria, I have only fond memories. Of course I remember the grass mattresses that were hard to sleep on, the leaky roofs that woke us in the middle of the night, the outside toilets (a deep hole in the ground surrounded by large wooden logs), getting stuck on the muddy roads and sleeping in the car with mosquitoes chewing on us all night.

"I remember these things well, but they were nothing compared to the fellowship with the Africans. They were my friends! We ate roasting ears around the fire at night. They took me into their lives and into their homes and treated me like one of them. Now they are all grown men and some of my best friends. Some of those boys are now pastoring churches. Some of those old friends have passed through Holland on their way to America to get a better education. What pleasure we had as we talked together about boyhood experiences!

Student preaching in the marketplace

"I think about them as boys who taught me Ibo and to whom I taught English. Now, they are men in the Lord's work. I'm so glad that I had a part in those very early years of my life in Africa.

"Mom, I think of your giving up so much of your time to teach me — many hours, days, and years to see that I got a good education. I remember reading for the first time and your being so happy about it.

"Years later when American History seemed so hopeless, you had the happy thought of asking Ray Brock (a missionary in the Bible school) to help me with this dull subject. He made it alive for me, and I learned to take an interest in subjects I didn't like.

"Dad, you'll never know how happy I was when you returned after being away visiting the churches. I know that this was your work, but I always hated to see you leave. When you came home, how happy I was! Do you remember playing Chinese checkers with me, or Tiddly Winks on the dining room table? Or when we went golfing together in Port Harcourt? I know now that you had to have a lot of patience for the little boy who trailed along behind you, but you always seemed happy to have me with you. I remember you let me shoot your gun at some hawks one day. I missed them, but I always remember that you allowed me to shoot your gun.

"Thanks, Mom and Dad, for allowing me to be a part of your lives and ministry. Now we have three boys of our own, and we are trying to raise them to value the same important things in life which I learned so many years ago. Dad, I even remember some of the sermons you preached. Many times I didn't know what you were talking about, but I learned through the years to get a little grasp of the Scriptures and the explanation of the Scriptures that you gave.

"As I grew older, I knew that God wanted me to be a missionary, only I was afraid I could never preach as freely as you did. Then God told me I would be a teacher. From then on, all I ever really wanted to do was to teach the Word of God in Bible school. God has given me that privilege. I never wanted anything more than to be a better teacher of the Word. I haven't succeeded as I wanted to. There is always more that I must learn. There are always better ways to express the truths that I have conquered thus far, but I'm happy doing what God wants me to do with my life. Now all I want for my boys is that they find the will of God for their lives, and that they do the will of God with all of their hearts."

In 1985 God called Don home. Theola continues in missionary service, and their sons Shawn and Chad are preparing for the ministry.

Don, Shawn, Theola, Chad, and Bradley Phillips, 1967

CHAPTER SIX

Confronting Heathenism

The God of Elijah — and of Gabriel

Gabriel Oyakhilome was born in Benin Province, far from any Christian influence, and grew up worshiping the gods of his father. At an early age he became a gardener for the High Commissioner of Nigeria in Enugu. One of the employees became sick and called on an Assemblies of God pastor for help. Miraculously, he was healed in answer to prayer. As a result Gabriel became deeply interested and began attending the Assembly in Enugu. What he heard led to his conversion and to his baptism in the Holy Spirit.

Gabriel became concerned about the salvation of his family back in EkoEwu. Although the Commissioner offered him more money if he would stay on, he gave up his job, obeyed the call of God on his life, and went back to tell his people about his new-found joy.

With Gabriel's deep commitment to God, his ministry was blessed through the years. His simple belief in God's promises and his acting on his belief drew people to the gospel. Soon a church was formed, consisting mostly of his relatives who had seen miracles of healing in answer to Gabriel's prayer.

One day some people in a neighboring town who had been became desperately sick from food poisoning. For one whole night Gabriel read the Scriptures and prayed for them. Even though they were extremely ill, some left when he asked them to give up their idols and trust in Christ. One by one those who rejected Gabriel's plea and left died that night. By morning those who remained with Gabriel had recovered. They went all over town telling what God had done for them. Soon a church was started and a building erected. Today there is a large church in this small town.

On another occasion Gabriel and the Christians in the town showed that the God of Elijah still answers prayer and puts to shame the heathen deities. They were erecting a school building with sun-dried mud blocks. The village chiefs had promised to help, for they wanted the school. However, when the work was to be done, they were absent.

Working long and hard, the church people finished the walls but lacked the bamboo framework for the roof and the mats to cover it, when a heavy rain came. Part of the wall fell, for sun-dried bricks can fall apart when they get wet. So, the Christians called a special prayer meeting and asked God to hold back the rains until they could completely finish the roof.

Now it was the rainy season, so rains should have been falling every day, but they stopped. Farms sown were suffering. The villagers called a meeting to see what could be done. The witch doctors came with their magic. For three nights they danced and called on their gods to send rain, but none came.

One of the chiefs said he knew what was wrong: the Christians were praying that there would be no rain. So the whole village came to Gabriel and asked him and his people to stop praying for no rain. Gabriel said they could not do that until the roof was on and reminded the chiefs of their promise to help.

The very next day, as the Christians were working on

their school, men came from every direction with bamboo, rope, and mats. The whole village had turned out to help complete the roof. By evening the job was done, at a great saving of money for the church.

That same night, after the people returned to their homes, it began to thunder. A few hours later the heaviest rain they had seen in months fell. The God of Elijah had once again shown that He was in charge of the elements!

Other miracles took place in Gabriel's ministry and churches were established as a result. God was training a leader who would be General Superintendent of the Assemblies of God of Nigeria for eleven years (1971-1982). Today there are thousands of people who are saved and filled with the Spirit in more than 200 churches in Benin Province (now Midwest State) where Gabriel took the gospel to his own people.

Watching Pagan Ceremonies

I thought maybe one heathen ceremony I saw was going to be my last as I ran for my life from the enraged dancers. I knew that some tribes made marimbas out of bamboo. That night I heard one for the first time. I was visiting the town of Eko-Ewu, and staying in the new house of Gabriel Oyakhilome's brother. About 9:00 p.m. I heard drums and another instrument.

Although it was the dark of the moon, I thought I could follow the sound and find the marimbas. As I walked along the dark road, the music became very loud and seemed to be coming from above the road. So I climbed the ten-foot high bank and found myself surrounded by dancing men, many carrying spears and machetes. Some of those spears were inches from my face, held by angry men. I had blundered in where I was not wanted. Edging my way back to the road bank, I slid and stumbled down the road, followed by a large group of angry men. When I was finally inside the house, I locked the doors and windows. All during the night the house was stoned. As the rocks hit the corrugated zinc roof, they made a dreadful din.

When it was daylight things quieted down. Gabriel, his brother, and the town chief with some of his counselors came to apologize for what had happened. I had walked in on a meeting of a heathen society and angered them. I told the chief and elders of my interest in the musical instrument and requested that they apologize for me and explain to the angry men that I had no desire to trouble them.

That was the only time I ever heard a marimba played close at hand. Though I heard it played again, always at night and far away, I never searched for it. I had learned my lesson!

However, that was not the only time I saw a heathen ceremony. The results were far different when I watched the ceremony at the sacred tree in the middle of the road about five miles (eight kilometers) from the Bible school in Umuahia. It was about seven feet in diameter. When the surveyors were laying out the road, they thought it would be easy to cut the tree down. But then they learned that this tree was an important god — or, rather, that an important god lived in that tree. The people in that area made sacrifices to the tree every year. The road builders, realizing its importance, simply left the tree where it was and built the road around on both sides of it.

One day when returning to Umuahia, I found hundreds of people all dressed up and watching while their elders danced around the tree. There was no way to pass; so I became one of the interested onlookers.

The old men moved slowly around the tree. Then a white chicken was handed to one of them. He cut the neck of the chicken and let the blood flow freely on the tree, plucked white feathers from the chicken, and spread them on the blood. They repeated this procedure three or four times until blood and feathers were all around the tree. Finally the ceremony broke up.

One young man that knew me by sight came and greeted me. I told him I was interested in what this ceremony was all about. "I know it is important," I stated, "since there are so many people present and all are dressed up. Also I see there have been several sacrifices offered to the tree."

He replied, "This is the most important blood sacrifice of my people, and we do this every year."

"You know, the people in the Bible used to offer blood sacrifices," I said. "Their high priest went alone into the presence of God once every year for the sins of the people. They had to continue this year after year."

The young man nodded and said, "That's just like our town. For every year as long as I can remember they have made this sacrifice that you've just seen."

"God got tired of the same sacrifice year after year," I replied, "and finally gave one last sacrifice to do away with all sacrifices of animals and birds. He gave His Son to die. After three days His Son rose from the dead; now no other sacrifices are needed for men and women who accept Him as the Savior for their sins. If they make a mistake and sin again, all they have to do is ask for forgiveness, and God will forgive them because of His Son's sacrifice."

"Oh," he said, "now I know who you are. One of your churches is down the road, but it's too far away. I've been there and have heard about Jesus. Why can't we have a church in our own town where our people would be able to hear what you have just told me?"

So I made a trip to that village and secured permission for a place for services. After making arrangements for a building, I sent one of our Bible school students to hold services. Today, after many years, we have a good church in that village. While some people may still sacrifice to that tree, at least no one there can say he has not heard of the better way — the way of Jesus Christ.

Taboos

In my travels I met people who would not eat fish, even though a large river went through their town. A pagan priest had decided fish was a "no-no" for a certain family or person.

Paul referred to the heathen customs of his day and their rules of "touch not, taste not, handle not." We found similar taboos — things that were forbidden by the heathen priests or by tradition. There were many taboos against eating certain foods. Some applied to a whole tribe; some only to an individual.

Dorothy met this problem when she taught the young Ibo mothers to eat oranges and to give orange juice to their babies. In one clan there was a taboo which forbade eating any citrus fruit. "One reason we don't eat oranges," the mothers told her, "is that they give our babies worms." She recognized that orange juice helped purge the worms from the babies. When the mothers saw the worms, they blamed the orange juice. Citrus trees grew everywhere, the people could eat all the other fruit, but oranges were forbidden.

Dorothy faced another taboo when she taught the mothers to feed their young children soft-boiled eggs. Eggs were plentiful and cheap and could improve their limited diet. The heathen priest had taught that feeding eggs to children would cause them to be thieves when they grew older. The Christian women were willing to defy this taboo, although the older heathen women gave them much opposition. It was a happy day for the children when they were able to eat eggs!

Idols and Jujus

"Heathenism" and "paganism" are broad terms referring to the ways of idolatrous people. Heathenism is not one practice but many. Some tribes have certain types of heathen customs that are very terrible. Basically, paganism is a belief in many gods — all nature, trees, the ground, fruits, everything that pertains to the natural world. Even the sun and moon can be worshiped. There are thousands of objects of worship. So-called gods in the area where we worked were made of wood, mud, or metal. Some were carved crudely. Some were mere rocks or sticks.

Jujus were associated with their gods and worship. Sometimes "juju" meant almost the same as "idol," but more often a juju was an amulet or object used for protection against evil spells or to cast spells on enemies.

Witch doctors made a big business out of preparing these jujus and using incantations to give them power. Sometimes a family's many objects of worship, idols, and jujus would fill a good-sized room. All were obtained at great cost.

When a pagan received the Lord as Savior, he had to dispose of all his idols and jujus publicly. The church people all assisted, for this man was making a declaration of his faith in Jesus Christ. Sometimes the heathen priests were indignant at this backsliding of their people, especially when they publicly burned their objects of pagan belief.

These objects might number in the hundreds, because there was a juju for every problem. If the person was having a difficulty, the pagan priest would go through a series of incantations and finally make an object that was to be tied around the neck of the person having the problem. The juju could be buried in the kitchen if the wife was not cooking good food, tied to the roof if it leaked, or put on the farm land so it would produce better crops.

When a person became a Christian, he and the church

members had to go wherever the jujus had been placed,

Jujus brought to be destroyed

bring them and any other "sacred" objects from the house to an open place to be burned publicly.

No one would light the fire but the man who was giving his life to God. We insisted on this. We were not simply disposing of his idols and jujus at his request; we wanted him to cut the line clean. We might pour kerosene on mud and bones, as they weren't very combustible, but he himself must light the match and start the fire. Finally, as the fire began to consume the pile of idols and jujus, the Christians rejoiced and clapped their hands in victory. They praised the Lord, for a newborn child of God was declaring to his heathen neighbors that he was no longer a heathen. Now he was worshiping the one true God!

Finding a "God"

Some of the heathen gods are living creatures. I remember the experience of one missionary who was trying to raise chickens. As fast as the eggs hatched, the chicks vanished. The missionary lived in a housing complex in a large city. The owner provided a watchman who came and slept on the premises. He was a likeable old man, but it was almost impossible to converse with him. He spoke little English. Whenever I visited I would talk to him in my language, and he talked to me in his. We would both smile a lot and shake hands.

One afternoon, sitting on the back veranda, I saw this old man moving some boxes and barrels about in a shed attached to the house. He was excited about something and called for me to come see what he had found. There, coiled neatly in a large box was a python four or five inches thick and at least five feet long. He quickly covered the box and went to his house. I assumed he was going to get a machete or a spear with which to kill the snake. So, to help make certain that it didn't get away, I found a long, heavy stick and sharpened the end with my knife.

When the watchman returned, he was not carrying a machete or spear, just a large bag. I showed him the weapon I had made. He was unhappy to see I was planning to use the stick on the snake. Carefully he put the python into his bag and carried it away over his shoulder. An hour later he came back with an empty bag. When the missionaries came out of the house, I told them about the snake in a box near their porch. Now they knew what had happened to their chicks!

Then the watchman explained to the missionary that his people worshiped pythons, so he couldn't kill it! He had taken it outside the city and turned it loose. After all, you don't kill the gods you worship!

Human Sacrifice and Cannibalism

"Go look on my veranda," District Officer Shute told me. There his floor was covered with pieces of a human body. Blood was everywhere. The people had found this human sacrifice in the bush, brought it, and laid it on the officer's veranda in the middle of the night or early morning, and left, for they didn't want to be involved in the investigation of the killing.

Although we had turned away from the churches in the Calabar Province, I made repeated trips back to Ikot Ekpene, hoping for some change, which did not happen for years. In these visits I had become acquainted with Mr. Shute, the District Officer and had a standing invitation to dine with him.

Now he explained that such human sacrifices were common occurrences. He had demanded that the people who found the bodies leave them where they were; then he would send the police to pick up the remains and bury them. But the practice continued of bringing the bodies, even in pieces, to his veranda.

Sometimes people were killed in order to eat certain parts of the body in a sacred ceremony. This was not for food, but to obtain power, or as a requisite in their worship. Certain secret societies had this practice. Although it was prohibited by law, cannibalism was common in various parts of Africa. Little was said about it. If the people talked about it among themselves, they never wanted to discuss it with or around white people, for it was recognized as the worst practice in heathenism.

On one occasion I was invited to meet with some national church leaders in northern Nigeria. The tribe in that area was much more war-like than the Ibos. I drove into town in the evening and went to the government rest house, where my cook and I put up my camp cot and mosquito net and ate a little lunch.

I expected some men to visit me that evening but no one came. The next morning there still was not a person to be seen as I walked into town. Usually every market place is jammed with people in the morning, but the market place was dead — no lorries (trucks) bringing people and produce to the market, no goods on display

— no one was there! The town was empty. Even the employees of the government rest house were gone.

The whole day passed with no one coming to see me. Early the next morning, before I got out of bed, an employee of the rest house knocked on my door. He told me that he knew men had planned to come see me but they were afraid, as was the whole town. He said, "I believe they will come later in the day."

He told me that their paramount chief had died, and his people were looking for persons to "send with him" on his journey. Then I learned that in this tribe when an important chief died it was the custom to kill a number of people to go with him and serve him in his after life. Would you believe that there were no volunteers for this service to their chief?!

From the early history of Nigeria came horrible stories of countless numbers of slaves sacrificed to pagan gods. The arrival of the British government outlawed this, and at least suppressed the practice. However human sacrifices were still being offered at the time we were there.

The Leopard Society

In the area where we lived there was a revival of the ancient, heathen Leopard Society. It was the worst of the secret societies in Nigeria. When a member of the Leopard Society goes on a murder mission, he wears iron claws over his fingers. Always he attacks his victim from behind on a lonely trail. He tears the jugular vein and catches the blood for certain ceremonies. Next, he cuts off the head, to be used in religious rites, and claws the body to give the impression that a leopard killed the person.

Over 200 persons were murdered in a small area of southeastern Nigeria in little more than a year. Living in the center of that area, Rex constantly heard reports about the Leopard Society. Authorities publicly hanged 20 of its members who were found guilty of murder. Still the

Society continued to terrorize the district. The English government sent police, and the local force was increased. But there was something mysterious and sinister behind the whole thing which made it difficult to stamp out.

Facing Danger

With the rise of the Leopard Society, other heathen societies began to renew old practices. Human heads were in demand as jujus. Since there were no more slaves to be sacrificed, everyone was in danger.

One of our pastors, James Nwoji, was riding along the road on his bicycle when he was attacked from behind. His assailant tried to cut off his head with one stroke of his long knife, but only succeeded in wounding him severely. James was wearing an old-fashioned sun helmet which partly deflected the blow. Some people came along and carried him to the hospital. The doctors said he could live only a short time. Soon some of our Christians heard of the attack and began to pray. God wonderfully undertook, and James Nwoji recovered. He bore for the rest of his life a long, light-colored scar from behind his ear to the point of his jaw where the flesh and bone had been cut. God had marvelously spared his life!

As soon as Pastor James was fully recovered and able to resume his duties, he came before the Executive Committee and offered to go wherever they might send him. He could have chosen to stay among his people where he would feel safe from another attack, but he wanted to be where God needed him.

Talking to an Idol

On one of my journeys to visit the churches I tried to take a shortcut and lost the way. I stopped in a little town to ask directions. The people gathered around from everywhere. One young man spoke English. He came forward with a smile and said, "Welcome, Sir. May I help you?"

"I want to get to the ferry, but I'm not going in the right direction. Will you please help me find the road?" I asked. By this time more than 100 people had gathered, all asking questions of the English-speaking young man. When he explained my problem, they all talked at once, telling him the best way for me to go. Then one of them brought me a chair, and I shook hands with everyone. Obviously they saw few travelers.

I was thirsty and wanted to buy some oranges. An older man gave a few short orders. In no time oranges and coconuts were brought to me in a head pan.

While refreshing myself, I looked around at the houses and noticed something different about them. On both sides of every front door were two wooden carvings about four feet tall. On one side was that of a man; on the other, that of a woman. I asked my English-speaking friend who these people were that the carvings represented. He acted as my interpreter as one of the older men gave me their names. "They are our town's gods and are there to protect and take care of each family," he explained.

I stood up, walked to the idols on the nearest house, and held out my hand as if to shake hands. The old man put his hand over his mouth in amazement and said, "I'm sorry, but they can't shake hands."

"But I see they both have hands," I said. "Since they can't shake hands, I'll just greet them." Standing in front of the male idol, I bowed politely and said, "Good morning, Sir." Everything was deathly quiet, and the god did not speak.

I turned to the carving of the woman, bowed again, and said, "Good morning, Madam." No answer. Now I had their attention. Through my interpreter I spoke, "They have hands and can't use them. They have mouths and can't speak. This morning before I left Eko-Ewu I talked to my God. He told me He would be with me on my long journey home. I asked Him to please be with my wife and son and take care of them while I was gone. I asked Him to go with me and lead me. He has led me here. I thought I was lost, but I wasn't. He brought me here to see you and visit your town."

Never have I spoken to a quieter, more attentive group. I asked if I could read to them from God's book. Taking my Bible from the car, I read slowly, using my interpreter, what God says about forgiveness of sin, Christ's death on the cross, His resurrection, and ascension to His Father.

After I finished, a flood of questions came, until I had to leave. When I asked if they would like me to send a man to stay with them and answer all their questions, with one voice they responded: "Yes!"

Circumstances made it impossible for me to return to that village — one of more than a thousand in that area. Repeated efforts by Bible school students to find it were in vain. In tears I have asked myself, "Why didn't I write down the name of the town and draw a simple map showing the way to it from Asaba?" To my knowledge, not one of our people ever found it. I could only pray that someone would witness for Christ to these people whose wooden gods could neither speak nor shake hands with me.

The Unknown God

In most African languages there are names for hundreds of idols and jujus. There is even a name for a God that is above all other gods. Somewhere in their past, someone told their grandfathers about a God of all gods who lived far away in the heavens and would never trouble them. This god was not known personally; and since he would not hurt people, they didn't have to make sacrifices to him. He made no demands on them. It was the lesser gods they feared — the ones who caused sickness, disaster, and death. They made idols or fetishes of these lesser gods, and offered sacrifices to them to appease their anger.

Whenever I visited a new tribe, with a language that was new to me, I insisted on learning their name for that God above all other gods. Usually I would have to appeal to the older men.

"Yes," they would say, "my grandfather told us there was a God like this who loves us and never troubles us." Then one would tell me his name, and the other old men would agree. They didn't know this God. They had no fear of him nor any association with him.

I thought of Paul as he viewed the many idols on Mars Hill and the inscription to the Unknown God. Paul said, "He is the One I declare unto you." So, we used this as a model many times in preaching to the heathen. We explained that this God above all gods was the one we had come to tell them about.

Many believed and were glad to have a teacher come to their village to tell them more. Some turned from their lifeless idols and accepted the true and living God. They came to know and love Him personally who so long had been for them the Unknown God.

CHAPTER SEVEN

Teaching Them . . . All Things

"Send us someone to teach us," had been the plea of the first Pentecostal Christians in Nigeria. So, we had come to teach — to obey Christ's command: "Go . . . teaching them to observe all things that I have commanded you." We taught in the churches and Bible schools. We taught others to teach, and sent them out to teach the children and plant churches. The Nigerian church became a teaching church.

Teaching them all things

As I visited the churches I felt, and the Nigerian leaders agreed, that we should plan for regular Bible school training. We decided to begin classes, even though no school buildings had been erected and we didn't know where the permanent location would be.

Umuahia was a center of activities, on the railroad, and had the missionary house. It seemed the logical location for the Bible school. The pastors would come for a month of classes, then return to their churches for a month. Every other month would be a Bible school month. With this arrangement it became evident that we should move from Port Harcourt to Umuahia; so we did.

The church served as a classroom. A crude dormitory was built behind the pastor's house in the church yard and the pastors slept on mats on the hard mud floor.

Some of the students were schoolteachers, some had a few years of schooling, and some could neither read nor write. The one uniting and redeeming feature was *desire*. These men wanted to be better ministers of the gospel. They had an all-consuming desire to read better, write better, and know God's Word better.

One thing I learned early: the lack of formal education didn't limit a man's knowledge of God or his experience with God. Some of the men who couldn't read well had a depth of experience in God and a grasp of the scriptures that was amazing to me.

George Alioha (a schoolteacher before entering the ministry) and I taught Bible, Doctrine, Pastoral Theology, Personal Evangelism, and Hermeneutics. We added other subjects as necessary in the following years, including Bookkeeping. Dorothy tutored some in English. George taught in English and supplemented in Ibo. I taught in English as George interpreted into Ibo. To know how we were doing, we gave frequent tests, using oral exams for those who couldn't write.

Learning seemed impossible for some. They could use their Ibo Bibles and preach simple sermons, but answering questions was most difficult. One day I heard George tell a man, "Think that you are preaching on this subject. What would you say?" After listening for a few minutes, George laughed and said, "You have answered the question and more! In the future think you are preaching and answer the question that way."

Night after night my heart overflowed with joy as I reviewed the day's classes with Dorothy. I taught for years in both Nigeria and America, but those first months were the best of all!

Learning Outside of Classrooms

The learning in Bible school was a two-way experience. Dorothy and I were learning about a culture foreign to us. We probably learned more in the evening informal discussions than in classes. In rainy weather these took place in the church. In dry weather they were held in the yard. We placed a gasoline pressure lamp on the ground and sat in a circle around it. The sky was the limit in the discussion topics. Students were full of questions about America, and we had many questions about their culture.

Sometimes hatching flying ants interrupted our talks. Thousands flew from their holes in the ground around our lamps. At first Dorothy and I felt this was a hindrance and were unhappy at the interruption. Then we learned that they were a source of food. Quickly the students gathered containers, filled them with water, and put them around the lamp. As the ants fell into the water, they were caught. All that was needed was to fry them, and they were good "sweet chop!"

Our winter weather in America was a never-ending source of interest to these people so close to the equator. The great mystery of ice, water as hard as cement, weather so cold that you saw your breath, or snow falling-these concepts were hard to grasp.

These evening discussions covered all areas of our doctrine, the use and control of the gifts of the Spirit, Sunday school, youth work, the differences in their form of worship and that practiced in America. We learned that some things which we considered wrong were approved by our Ibo Christians. But there was no question about the sinfulness of idols, jujus, blood sacrifices, polygamy, child marriages, and immorality.

One custom that seemed wrong to us was that of paying a bride price. This seemed to us like buying a girl like any piece of property. But here for a young couple to agree to marry without the process of discussion between their families, agreement on a bride price, and its payment would be no marriage at all. No civil or church ceremony could take the place of this custom. Any couple bypassing the payment of the bride price was considered by the Christians to be living in sin. If either one was a member of the church, he or she was excommunicated immediately.

The innate politeness of the people, the honor they gave to all older people and those in authority, their desire to establish Christian homes-these were wonderful parts of their culture. Their home life, however, was quite different from ours in many ways. They were amazed to see me eat with my family and to see us talk, read, or play games together as a family. We learned, to our amazement, that the culture of the people in Bible times was much more closely related to the African culture than to the American culture.

Eventually we talked about drinking beer and wine. This was from the palmwine trees. The farmer taps the tree and lets the liquid sit for several hours in the sun. Then it becomes a potent drink, and an even stronger liquor when it is run through a still. Our pastors had grown up tapping palm wine trees and drinking "tombo," the Ibo name for palm wine. Few if any restrictions had been imposed by European missions, so almost everyone imbibed.

It would have been easy for me to guide or even dictate what to do, but I felt it was essential for them to lead in this discussion. One evening one of the older men spoke of palm wine and its effect on those who drank it. He felt a decision should be made for the pastors and then for all our members.

Matthew Ezeigbo stated that he had come to the point a year before that he would no longer drink palm wine. "At one time I felt I should limit my drinking to two cups a day. But I found that palm wine spoiled my arithmetic — two cups became three, then three became four, and then I lost count. As for me, I will never drink strong drink again."

Others spoke in a similar vein. Finally the decision was made to strongly disapprove of drinking palm wine by any of our ministers, and to immediately begin teaching our members total abstinence, which was to become our standard.

And so, we all learned, bonds of friendship were strengthened, and God was changing lives both in and out of the classroom at Bible school.

Rise and Build!

A permanent Bible school called for adequate buildings — not just the cramped quarters of a crowded church. And so, before we moved to Umuahia we applied for land and drew plans for the buildings.

The site on top of a hill overlooked beautiful valleys on three sides. To make the sun-dried mud blocks, workers carried many gallons of water on their heads up a steep hill from the nearest source of water, a spring at the bottom of the hill.

We had no difficulty in hiring people for the work during the season when they weren't farming. I hired as many as 50 young men and young women to carry water, to trample the mud, and to make it into blocks. First they loosened a portion of the ground with a shovel, removed the rocks, poured on water, then worked and trampled it until it became soft mud. What fun some of the girls had as they sang, jumped, and danced in the mud until it became the proper consistency! Then the men shoveled it into hinged wooden molds. They let it dry for a day in the sun, then took off the molds and let the blocks dry thoroughly. We made more than 10,000 of these 8"x10"x18" sun-dried bricks.

I made a wheelbarrow so the workers wouldn't have to carry the blocks on their heads. But pushing the wheelbarrow was harder for them than carrying heavy loads, as they were used to, on their heads!

We used iroko wood for the door frames, window frames, and the wall plate to which the roof is attached. This wood is so hard it had to be chiseled instead of planed. Using such hard wood proved very valuable, as the termites had great difficulty in chewing it and eating it. These pests would have eaten the frames of softer wood like ice cream!

The lumber was so hard that nails couldn't be driven into it, so split bamboo was tied on in overlapping rows. The roof was then covered with mats that served as shingles. It would turn water for a couple of years and then would need constant repairs until it had to be completely replaced. It's much better to use galvanized roofing (which the termites can't eat).

The cement for the floor was a very poor grade, and we had to resurface the floor later. However, the urgency of the need demanded immediate action. We got the best materials available, and, like the men led by Nehemiah, met the challenge to "rise up and build"!

Whenever workmen took part in a building project like this, they all brought something to plant, which served as a marker to show that they had a part in the building. So, they planted fruit trees all around the Bible school property and missionary residence. In each deep hole left from taking out the dirt for the blocks they set out 10 or 20 banana plants. Later we could pick a stalk of bananas from ground level. The school and faculty enjoyed oranges, lemons, limes, and bananas from the trees the workers had given as a reminder of their appreciation for their Bible school.

My experience in building the Bible school and our house helped win my special Ibo name. Shortly after arriving in Nigeria, we learned about the custom in all the tribes of naming the new missionaries. After becoming acquainted with them, they give them a name which indicates some outstanding characteristic, good or bad. I asked our pastor and the employees in our house what my name was. They answered, "It is too early yet. Our people don't know you yet."

Months passed, then our cook and houseboy reluctantly gave me the names of several white people, for they were not all complimentary. In my notes of many years ago I found a list of names given to people we knew. In English they meant:

> The lady with straight eyes and a soft heart.
> The missionary who loves our children.
> The missionary who counted the matches.
> The storekeeper who couldn't count.
> The missionary who loved God's book.
> The missionary full of questions.
> The man who hated his family.
> The small man who was a big man.

While we were building our home and Bible school, I worked with the men at all kinds of tasks. I learned to make and lay mud blocks, and carried them on my shoulder, to the amusement of the young people. I even helped the carpenter cut the 2x6 ceiling beams. It was most uncommon for a white man to do such labor.

One morning I asked Richard, our cook, "Have the

people given me a name yet?" He was evasive in his reply, so I pressed him for an answer. Reluctantly he said, "Yes, and I don't like it! They have named you 'the white man who works.'" Usually white men hired Nigerians to do all the manual work.

Then I told Richard that American children did many kinds of work with their hands, then when they were older they worked in part-time jobs to help them get an education. I mentioned that I had held a variety of jobs. I sold newspapers at seven years of age, and later worked with cement in a large building project. Only when they saw that all the other American missionaries did all kinds of work in the missionary program did they begin to understand.

"Can't the Women Learn?"

Dorothy recognized that our women, not only in Port Harcourt and Umuahia but in all our churches, needed Bible training and practical help for their homes. So, she proposed that we hold a two-week session for women. She continued to have women's classes on the local church level. Then she announced in several of the churches that all the women were invited to a session of their own at the Bible school. I passed the information on to the churches I visited.

However, the pastors were concerned. Some talked to Dorothy personally. Some wrote to her saying, "Madam, we thank you for your love for our women. But we think you are making a mistake. You are new. You do not understand our women. Our women do not have any sense. They can't be taught; they cannot learn. You will be wasting your time, and we fear you will become discouraged with all the people in Nigeria. And so we are writing in love to warn you that this program may prove a great disappointment."

Dorothy was undaunted by what these well-meaning

men told her. God had laid this work on her heart when she was a schoolgirl. She was more determined than ever to prove to all the Nigerian men that, given a chance, these women could learn! Perhaps God took up the challenge, too, for they were His creation.

Dorothy had found the women in Port Harcourt and in Umuahia bright and receptive to teaching, even though most had never had one day in school. Although women weren't considered on a par with men. many showed great wisdom in business. They were the money makers in many homes. Dorothy was determined to give them the opportunity to learn in Bible school.

And so they came! On the day after the men finished their Bible school session, the women began to arrive, young and old, from all over Iboland. Some had walked for two or three days, stopping at night with relatives or friends on the way. Some were even carrying children! All had to bring food, for they must feed themselves while in Bible school. This was a new thing, not only in their personal lives, but also in Nigeria — a Bible school for women!

God made that two-week school a great blessing, not only because of its immediate effect on the students, but also for its long-lasting effect on the churches and districts. Almost with reluctance the men agreed that this first school for women was a great success. Their women had been able to learn. Some of the women had brought unsaved friends, hoping that God would meet their need. Some of these were saved and some received the baptism in the Holy Spirit.

The work among the Nigerian women far exceeded our expectation. They readily accepted responsibility, even in sharing the gospel in neighboring towns. Groups of women from a single church or from several churches would go into one town to witness to the women and pray for them. When they found women or children who were sick or in need they ministered to them, cooking, cleaning, being real angels of mercy. Of course the people asked, "Why are you doing these things for us who are strangers?" As a result of the women's ministering in love and telling the people of God's grace, a new church was born in that town.

Today the women in our churches are strong pillars and used greatly in building the church in Nigeria. How glad they are that someone insisted they should have a chance to learn! Many things that Dorothy taught about health and hygiene are now taught in the public schools. On our last visit to Nigeria in 1982, some women, grandmothers now, came to Dorothy with their families and spoke of that first wonderful school for women of almost half a century ago!

"Don't Give Me High Grades!"

In the following years, the Nigerian Bible College became co-educational. God has shown the wisdom through the years of our integrating the women in our educational program. Husbands and wives now sat together in Bible school, taking the same exams. The women demonstrated that they "had sense."

To the consternation of some of the men, these women earned good grades and at times even excelled their husbands! This could create problems. We remember one bright young woman in Bible school with her husband. She begged the teachers not to grade her higher than her husband. "Please," she said, "if I get a higher grade than my husband, it will not make peace in our home." So, although she deserved a high grade, she received just a passing grade, no more.

"He Gave Some . . . Teachers"

A basic need for solid growth was for teachers — good teachers in the Bible school and trained teachers in the churches. Back in those early days our work grew faster than we anticipated, so we recruited Reuben Okeiyi to assist. As you recall, Reuben was the schoolteacher converted in our first service in Nigeria. Although English was the official language at that time, many had difficulty in speaking or writing it. So Reuben taught English for hours each day. He taught a preparatory year of basic studies so those who needed it could keep up with the class later in the regular studies.

As the work grew, more missionaries came and all were involved in teaching, in this school, in others that were opened, or in the local churches.

Many of those who graduated from the Nigerian Bible College, became excellent pastors and teachers. Several (including some from the preliminary course) went to Central Bible College or to the Assemblies of God Theological Seminary in Springfield, Missouri, to earn a Bachelor of Arts and advanced degrees. Some went for further studies to West Africa Advanced School of Theology in Lome, Togo.

Their advanced training helped prepare them to found or teach Bible schools in the various areas. Today, eight Bible schools and two graduate schools exist in Nigeria. Even so, there have never been enough pastors to meet the needs of all the new churches. Some pastors still do double or triple duty, with the aid of young people or women's groups.

"Please . . . a School in Our Town"

As the Assemblies of God grew, with churches being built in many towns, opposition also grew. Our people were harassed by the chiefs and the people. There was little I could do about it. One common harassment was putting the children of our believers out of school.

Public schools didn't exist in Nigeria at that time. All schools were operated by church mission groups. But some of these opposed the Pentecostals and wouldn't allow the children of our members to attend their schools. So, our pastors and members began to ask for their own schools.

If a church had the proper buildings and could employ qualified teachers, it could have a school. Anyone who had completed the Standard 6 education (8th grade) could obtain a teaching certificate from the government by applying for it through a mission.

After consulting with our national brethren and our other missionaries who had arrived by then, we set up guidelines. We would open a school provided that:

1) There was an Assemblies of God church in the town.
2) The church was fully supporting its program.
3) Students paid school fees at the standard level.
4) The church and town agreed to have the school under the direction of the mission's area school supervisor.
5) The teachers' monthly salary was met; failure to do so would result in closure of the school.
6) The mission, through the school supervisor, was the sole director of all matters pertaining to the school, and its only intermediary between the school and the Educational Department of the Nigerian government.
7) The church and the town jointly applied to open a school, and the town elders were informed as to their share of the cost of the buildings. Any expansion of these was the joint responsibility of town and church.
8) Only credentialed teachers approved by the Education Department were hired.

Two facts helped us decide to establish schools: the Nigerian government encouraged daily religious training in schools, and our Assemblies of God had full authority in establishing the curriculum for Bible classes. We began with simple elementary schools. Later we had Evangel High School, completely financed by the Nigerian churches

Our schools enjoyed the respect of the people and of the government because of the high standards we set for our teachers and students. Many towns applied for schools where we had no church. I answered them, "When there is an Assemblies of God church in your town able to support itself, on that day we will talk about a school, not before." My decision helped break down the opposition of some town elders who had refused to grant us permission to build a church, or where one had been burned to the ground. Now, with schools a possibility, attitudes began to change.

Since the school buildings were made of mud by the people, the only expense was the roof. If enough people shared the work, they could build a school. Some churches assumed the whole responsibility. Others appealed to the town elders for help. They usually desired a school in their town. But even with all the efforts of towns and people, there were never enough schools to meet the needs of all who wanted to attend. Even when a new school opened, it could accept only a limited number of children.

In those days there were no birth certificates. No one knew for sure how old a child was. The teachers had to decide which children were ready for the first grade. First, they turned away those who looked over six years old. I was amazed to see how they determined if child was old enough. They had him reach over the top of his head and touch the lobe of his ear. If he could do it, he was at least five years old and was accepted.

Each year hundreds were disappointed when their children couldn't get an education. If a boy reached the age of eight and hadn't gone to school, he was doomed to be illiterate unless someone tutored him.

The Picture Today

Over the years the picture has changed. The Assemblies of God has penetrated into many more areas of

Nigeria. In 1988 there are more churches — 3,052 churches and 250 outstations — under the care of 2,887 credentialed ministers and 734 layworkers. Some years ago the government nationalized all parroquial schools and now operates the elementary and high schools.

Correspondence ministry started by Esther Cimino and carried on by the International Correspondence Institute has taught half a million students courses ranging from evangelistic to ministerial training.

Teachers in eight Bible schools, two of which grant degrees, still help students find and follow God's will, still enjoy friendly discussion and spiritual refreshing, and are training 1,223 students in the Word so they will be "able to teach others also."

Central Bible College Students, Umuahia, 1960

CHAPTER EIGHT

What Do Superintendents Do?

Besides Preaching and Teaching

What is the national superintendent of the churches on a new field supposed to do? Supervise! This might mean everything from making mud blocks to representing the churches before the government. While the Bible school was our chief interest, there were many competing responsibilities. I visited the churches, preached in new areas, served as treasurer, advised pastors, and worked with the other Executive Committee members to develop the national church.

Counting Hands Under the Tablecloth

In the early days the churches all had a table with a tablecloth in front of the pulpit. At the time for the offering, each person would come forward, put his right hand under the tablecloth, and leave his offering there. Puzzled, I asked why they gave in this way. They quoted Matthew 6:3: "When thou doest alms, let not thy left hand know what thy right hand doeth." This was their way of giving secretly!

As the months passed, I began to suspect that more hands were put under the tablecloth than the pieces of money left there. So one day I counted everyone who came up. Then I stood nearby while the pastor and one or two of the men slowly counted the money. Sure enough, more people had gone forward than there were pieces of money. I did this several times, still coming to the same conclusion.

Another common custom among the young churches was the scurrying around to close doors and windows when prayer time was announced. Openings were covered with mats if there were no doors or windows. We prayed in darkness. When I asked why they did this. They answered me with Scripture again: "When thou hast shut the door, pray to thy father in secret."

During our next months of Bible school, the pastors gave me the same answers about these customs. I reminded them that Daniel prayed openly; his enemies saw him and reported him to the king for praying. The priests prayed openly before the people, and Jesus prayed outdoors where anyone listening could hear Him.

Then I brought up the problem about the number of hands put under the tablecloth. After that they made their own count, were shocked at the pretense of giving to God by many people, and changed the manner of taking up the offering — records of tithing. This marked a great change in the life of the churches.

Counting Cowry Shells

While I was pastoring in Illinois, I had a feeling that I was wasting time, or just marking time, until the Lord opened up the way for me to go to Africa. Actually, I was learning many things I would need to know in years to come. Very much against my will I became District Treasurer. Brother Bill Wood, who had held this office, gave me a one-day training in bookkeeping. I had never kept books in my life! It sounded easy, but many times my head ached from trying to balance the books at the end of the month.

I didn't know it, but that was a very definite part of my

training for Africa. Immediately upon my arrival, it became my responsibility to set up a bookkeeping system for the new Assemblies of God in Nigeria and act as field treasurer.

What complications! Nigeria used the British system of pounds, shillings, and pence, not a decimal system. The Portuguese had introduced the use of manillas (pieces of metal molded in the shape of a horseshoe) during the slave trade back in the 17th century. They were still in use in 1940. Each was usually worth an English penny. A man with $10 worth of manillas had about all he could carry.

Then there were the cowries — tiny mollusk shells often used for jewelry. Twenty-seven cowry shells were strung on a string, and twelve such strings were worth about one penny. They were the most common currency in the markets and made up, in bulk at least, a large part of the contributions to the churches. A bushel basket of cowries would be valued at fifty cents.

Most people in the interior used cowry shells and manillas; they were suspicious of the British pence and shillings. They didn't want the tenshilling note or a one-pound note, for to them paper was not money!

And one big problem for the bookkeeper was the fluctuation in value of the cowry shell and manilla. In the dry season thousands of people attended the markets, so buying and selling was brisk, and the value of manillas and cowries went up. In the rainy season business was slow, so their value went down. I had to include all this in my bookkeeping system!

Picture this if you can. The pastors of eleven churches came to our first account day. This was the day of the month when they were to bring in all church income except for small expenditures such as for kerosene, matches, or to repair a leaky roof. They brought the rest and placed it in a pile in front of me. There were stacks of cowry shells, manillas, and all kinds of loose change. There were half-pennies, pennies, shillings, three-pence, six-pence, and two-bob pieces worth two shillings. But no paper money.

I had to figure the total money that was before me for each church. The pastors helped me. We placed each type of money in a pile according to its value and then calculated the total. To complicate matters, there were offerings of chickens, eggs, or a goat. There hadn't been time to convert these into money. If you had been there on account day, you would think the church looked like a produce store. These offerings had to be valued and figured in. Great discussions were involved: How much does a goat of a certain size and guessed-at age cost in the market? Such items, as part of church income, surely required discussion.

Whatever the total was, we took one-tenth of the entire income as the church tithe and put it in the general fund. (I can look back and say God helped me with my arithmetic in those days!) Most of the balance went to the pastor. From the money designated as his salary, I would count out 10% as his tithe. This was added to the general fund along with the church tithe.

It took me all day to take care of the books on account day. A guide had been made as to the minimum salary a pastor should receive, according to the cost of living where he worked. Then when we knew what our total income was from tithes to the general fund, we helped those pastors receiving less than the minimum, trying to make up the balance from the general fund. At first what the fund gave was not enough, but it helped them to know that when they tithed and the churches tithed, the poor pastors would always receive some help in addition to what their church could pay.

Supervising the Tithes

The pastors and members alike had decided they would be required to pay tithes. At first I was reluctant to take a man's tithes from his salary on account day. However, the pastors had a clear idea of tithing. They said, "Brother Phillips, we have lived under a chief who, with his counselors, made all the important decisions for the people of the town. There were not many choices for us. We suggest you deduct the tithes from all the pastors at account day. If you add any money from the general fund to the account of any pastor, it too should be tithed."

"But," I asked, "what if some pastor refuses to have his tithes taken in this way?"

"Then," they said after discussing the problem, "that man should be given his whole salary, including his tithe, and he should be dismissed from the ministry. If one man is given the choice of not tithing while others are paying their full tithe to the district, only confusion will result."

And so it was written in the records that all ministers should pay their tithes on account day. If any man refused to tithe and demanded all his money, that day he was to resign from the Assemblies of God. He would be asked to vacate the parsonage, and a letter of explanation would be sent to the church.

And so, I advised the pastors to teach their people how to tithe. A date was to be set, and all members were to be informed that after that date their membership would be in question if they didn't tithe.

In the following months, giving in the churches grew to exceed the expenses and the pastor's salary. In this case, we pasted a receipt for the balance in the church record book. We held this balance in the church's name to be called on to meet its needs at a later date. If the pastor or church treasurer had kept the money hidden in his home, his house might be robbed. Since there were no banks in the villages, we held the money for the church in a central bank account and disbursed it as needed. The churches always knew how much they had on deposit.

Since many traveled in business and there was no consistent record of their tithes, a membership card was printed and given to each member. His name, address, and the name of his church were on the face of the card. On the folded part were 52 squares where the tithes were to be recorded and initialed as paid. The card served a dual purpose: identification as a member of the Assemblies of God wherever he went, and a record of his tithes for a full year.

As I write this today, those salaries of 46 years ago provided by the tithes seem unbelievably small. But members, pastors, and missionaries were building a new organization and wanted it on a solid, biblical foundation. An alternate plan used by some other denominations would have appealed for churches in America to support the pastors, but later we saw that they had many problems with this system. And although our system of tithing might not have seemed adequate at first, thank God that He blessed it and developed a strong, self-supporting national church.

Getting Land for Churches

One of my many duties as superintendent was to help new church groups get land for building. We wanted land in town instead of out in the bush. Land was never privately owned in many villages until plots were assigned to families. Unassigned plots belc ged to the village and were controlled by the town chief and his head men. If a pastor applied for land to build a church, the procedure became long and costly. The chiefs would do nothing without a gift. Sometimes they asked for what they wanted, even expensive things. However, when I visited them to apply for land for a church, they didn't request gifts.

My meeting with the chief and the town elders to request land was formal but cordial. No business was brought up immediately; that would be offensive. We sat together and talked first of the crops, the weather, our families, problems facing the town, and any sickness of importance. There were questions about my gold-capped front tooth. The Eastern Ibo people had beautiful teeth, took excellent care of them, and had never seen a cavity. They had never heard of a dentist and found it hard to believe that a man had put the gold on my tooth. It was of great interest to them.

Finally the town leaders would take me to some land and ask me to pick out what was needed. Sometimes a price was set, but usually it became a gift.

Building the church was the responsibility of the local Christians. Most were humble, but I saw that the Holy Spirit is no respecter of places any more than of persons. People were saved, filled with the Spirit, and taught the things of God in these humble places.

Interceding About Road Work

In those days we discussed and dealt with many problems that our members faced. One was cleaning the roads. Southern Nigeria receives an average 200 inches of rainfall a year. With the warm, muggy weather, grass and weeds grew rapidly in the dirt roads and soon covered them with tall vegetation.

Road gangs employed by the government took care of a few of the major roads, but the towns had to take care of the rest. The chief and his counselors decided on the days for this work and informed all the people. Men women and children were sent out to spend so many days cleaning the road. They cut down the fast-growing bushes and weeds and reopened the ditches.

The problem was that this work was done in honor of the heathen deities which supposedly controlled the roads. All those who cleaned the roads had to make offerings to these gods. On this point our Christians resisted. They applied Paul's advice about eating food offered to idols. They cleaned roads with all the town if there was no honoring of a heathen deity. But if a heathen god was consulted about the time, and the road was cleaned in honor of the gods, the Christians would take no part in it. Many went to jail because they refused to do so as a matter of conscience.

Many times some church would call for me to go to the chief and explain the situation. Our people were willing to clean the road; if given a certain portion they would clean more than what would be their share, but they refused to do it on the Lord's day or on the day appointed by a heathen god. Any other day they would work from morning to night cleaning the roads.

This was unacceptable to many chiefs, so I was called on to take the matter to the District Officer, an Englishman. Usually he would write a note absolving our people of cleaning roads on objectionable days, provided that they cleaned their part on other days.

Another problem was building the chief's house or caring for his affairs or farm, as these things too were done by the people at a time thought propitious to the idols. Again our people assured the chief they would do their part of the work, but not on the Lord's day or on the day appointed by a heathen deity. The chiefs found that putting our Christians in jail didn't help, for they went cheerfully, sang and witnessed to everyone in jail, making their stay a nuisance to others in jail and to the jailer.

Before it became known that the Assemblies of God was a "real Mission" with missionaries from America, persecution was common and sometimes violent. Homes were broken into and properties stolen. Our people never retaliated. As the Mission won the respect of the government, the attitude of local officials and people changed, and there was less persecution.

Accepting Change

As superintendent of the work in all of Nigeria, I had to travel a lot. I never knew I had a heart as far as any trouble was concerned until after three years of traveling, riding bicycles, walking up and down hills and through forests, and cutting trees that had fallen across the road in order to get to the churches. While I knew I had some physical difficulty, I assumed it was because of my strenuous program.

One day I discovered that all was not well. I had been invited to a church about ten miles from Enugu, the capital and government center of the Eastern Region. I drove to Enugu and rented a bicycle for the rest of my journey, for there was no proper road for a car. This narrow road was built on a dike. The fields on each side were at least six feet below its level. I had always ridden a bicycle without any difficulty, but this day I fell off time after time. I didn't hurt myself or have any distress with my heart, but for some reason I couldn't ride in a straight line.

I arrived at the church about 10:00 a.m. The service lasted till noon. I had decided to go right back to Enugu, but the pastor begged me to stay for the 2:00 p.m. service. We had a wonderful service. People were filled with the Spirit and some were healed in answer to prayer, but I was very tired.

At 4:00 p.m. I got on my bicycle to return to Enugu. I began to hurt inside and had to stop time after time to keep from falling. Still I didn't know what the trouble was. I only knew that cycling on the sandy roads or walking for miles between churches had become almost impossible for me.

Things culminated at our annual district council in

Umuokotawam. When the council was over and we were packing the car to go back to Umuahia, I found myself lying half inside the trunk of the car while Dorothy tried to help me back on my feet. We went back home, but I knew my time in Nigeria was limited.

The time arrived for Dorothy and me to go to the States on furlough in 1944. We were reunited with Don in Cleveland and had two weeks of vacation. I spoke in some services, but itinerating as missionaries usually do on furlough, was physically impossible for me.

A friend told me about a well-paying job in mechanical drafting. I had training in that field, but I had prayed too long and waited too long to be a missionary to give it all up now. I knew I could never give up the call of God for money.

God opened up the way for us to pastor a wonderful group of people in the Christian Assembly of Zion, Illinois, until 1951. Then He told us as we prayed, "It's time to return to Nigeria."

We arrived back during a council meeting in Umuahia. All my duties were handed back to me except the Bible School. However, there was a vast difference in the work, for now there were about 20 missionaries, and the national church leaders had grown and matured.

We set up our home in Port Harcourt, and gave ourselves to encouraging, assisting, and guiding the work of God in all of Nigeria until 1954. At that time I became Field Secretary of the Assemblies of God for Africa and continued with this work until 1971. We lived in Springfield, Missouri, but my travels all over Africa took me occasionally to Nigeria. My last visit there, with Dorothy, was in 1982. As we met old friends and rejoiced in the growth of the work, our minds went back to the early days and how the Lord had brought about such a wonderful change.

CHAPTER NINE

Reaching Out With the Gospel

Starting New Churches

What a happy privilege it was for Dorothy and me to live among a people who had a deep desire for the things of God and were not satisfied until thousands of others had an opportunity to know Jesus Christ.

Over the years since our arrival, about 100 Assemblies of God missionaries have been appointed to Nigeria. They have found cooperative, hard-working national pastors who went to any length to see the gospel preached all over Nigeria. As a result many Assemblies of God churches exist in Nigeria today.

From the beginning, each church able to support a pastor started a church in another town. If it could not provide a pastor for it, the pastor of the older church divided his time. The young people and others helped. Everybody, every church, was interested in reaching out, evangelizing, and starting new churches.

Layworkers and those saved and filled with the Spirit carried on as best they could in many of the new churches while waiting for the graduation of students from the Bible school to come and pastor them. Then they started other churches for the glory of God. This practice has been the secret of Nigeria's success. God's Spirit rested on the people.

Because of their drive and initiative, the Ibos as traders or working in the government were found in all areas of Nigeria. In every government department there were workers who spoke Ibo, people whose home was back where we lived. So, when we said we lived in Umuahia, many times we would hear in response, "That is near my home." Immediately a door opened for us. "This Gospel . . . to All"

While the work began among the Ibo people, it didn't stop with them. Some went to other tribes, learned their language, preached the gospel and developed God's work among these "foreign" people.

I remember some discussions of our national committee about tribes which had not heard the full gospel. We took the New Testament church as our example. In the New Testament:

1) Every book was written by a missionary.
2) Every letter to a church was to one on a mission field.
3) Every letter to an individual was to the convert of a missionary.
4) The one book of prophecy was to seven missionary churches in Asia.
5) The language is the missionary's language.
6) The problems which arose in the early church were largely problems of missionary procedures.
7) Of the 12 apostles chosen by the Lord, all became missionaries but one; he betrayed his Lord.

Like the early church, our Nigerian Christians had a missionary spirit. They determined to send workers wherever this gospel was not known, so that those in other tribes might become followers of Christ.

"Our Missionary, Ben"

Ben Osumo was loved by all his brothers in Christ. When the churches decided to send their first missionary to Abakaliki, Ben Osumo offered to go The Ibo churches gave offerings, clothes, and household equipment to Ben and his family. After prayer they sent him on his way. You would hear his name called in times of prayer. He was "our missionary."

Ben made a deep impression on the people to whom he ministered with his happy disposition and God's touch on his life. But the Nigerian church learned a solemn lesson — sometimes a great price has to be paid to spread the gospel. Before most of the churches heard of his need, Ben sickened and died. His friends became more consecrated and committed, recognizing that dedication to God for service, was no guarantee of a problem-free life. In the following months many young pastors offered themselves for missionary service.

Some went far north; others, far east and over the mountains into the Cameroons. Tribes who couldn't have heard the gospel from American missionaries heard it from national missionaries willing to dedicate their lives and resources to fulfill the command of Christ.

How happy we were to see the national church assume this responsibility! When our early American missionaries entered the Cameroons, they found numbers of full gospel churches in the mountains that separate Nigeria and the Cameroons. The Nigerian Christians, as an organized effort of the national church or on their own, had crossed the mountains and ministered the gospel until churches were established and developed under the leadership of their own people.

By Mammy Lorry to Western Nigeria

A thousand miles of dirt road from Umuahia to Lagos — and only four gallons of gas per month during wartime rationing! Dorothy and I decided to make the trip to encourage the churches in that area, but obviously we couldn't go in our car. So we went in a truck used as a bus, called a "lorry" by the British.

The people called them "mammy lorries," because so many women traveled on them taking their loads to markets. Seats in the open or canvas-covered back of the truck were planks across its width. Fortunately, we had seats in the cab.

Western Nigeria was not the homeland of the Ibo tribe, but there were four congregations of Ibos in Lagos and Ibadan. These people were employed by the government or large trading firms. On arriving, our Christians had immediately begun worship services in their homes and later went into rented buildings.

These four churches had grown and prospered. Living a thousand miles away, we had heard only occasionally of them. To our joy we found hundreds of believers worshiping God under the leadership of their own pastors. These had no special training but they read God's Word and had a vital experience with Him. No one was qualified to baptize the converts, and so they were not full members of the churches. But God had baptized many with His Holy Spirit, and they were evangelizing everywhere. As a result of this trip, we sent an older pastor to oversee this burgeoning work. Most of the pastors eventually went to Bible school and then returned to their ministry in Western Nigeria.

Visiting Peter in Ibadan

Some time before our visit to Lagos, Peter had worked in our home. He was a good young man who could read and write, was very pleasant and very helpful, but didn't seem to have any special talent.

Whenever I had to make a trip, I told Peter I was making him responsible for the care and safety of Dorothy and Donald. We put a mosquito net over the dining room table, and Peter unrolled his sleeping mat underneath it. There he slept with his spear and machete by his side about eight feet from our bedroom door. Woe be to anyone who might come in the night to try to harm Don or Dorothy! Sometimes students came to our house at night if they were ill or if people had arrived from a distance. Peter met them with his spear and machete. He was taking care of Madam and Donald!

One day Peter gave notice that he was going to leave us. His brothers in Ibadan had asked him to join them. They had started a church in that large city.

Peter and his brothers rented a room in a large compound for a meeting place. Picture a big square with houses built together on all sides of it. The center space served for the cooking fires, for resting in the evening in nice weather, and where the people lived when not shut away in their little apartments.

Through the middle of the room for services ran a 3-foot-deep, cement-lined ditch that carried all the sewage from this compound. Smaller ditches from each home emptied into this main channel which then ran out into a deeper gutter along the street. No such thing as underground sewer pipes existed in this big city!

This is where I preached when we made our trip to Western Nigeria! The odor defies description! While preaching I straddled the ditch, with the people out in front of me, some seated on one side and some on the other. Behind me sat Peter with a bottle of carbolic acid, dribbling it into the ditch to alleviate that horrible odor of the sewage.

That group of people became the nucleus of a very large church in Ibadan. As it grew, members were given the responsibility of starting churches in their part of town. It divided many times to start daughter churches. Several years later there were 20 churches in Ibadan. These attracted people from the tribes of Western Nigeria and extended our work to these people. Dorothy and I arrived back in Umuahia three weeks later, knowing more about the distance to the cities of Western Nigeria and

with a greater sympathy for those who traveled in dis-
comfort on a mammy lorry.

By Train to Kafanchan

A narrow-gauge railroad ran from Port Harcourt
through Umuahia and on north 1200 miles to Kano, then
southwest to Lagos. Many times I traveled by train, for
we had churches all along the railroad. Our traveling Ibos
who had gone into business or worked in every city along
the railroad were starting churches. Nathan Nwacuku, an
engineer on the train, had won many people to the Lord
all along his route. Among those filled with the Spirit in
the early outpouring, he had done much to support the
work in Port Harcourt.

The train had three classes. First class was for the elite
and was far too expensive for a missionary's budget. Third
class was cheap but unbelievably crowded with loads,
goats, pigs, and chickens, along with packed humanity.
The people had to carry with them all they needed, including food, on the three-day trip to the North. Eating
was a problem. The people spread their food on the floor

in the aisles and squatted around it while eating. Moving from your location in third class became almost impossible.

I usually traveled second class. Its cars had compartments for six people, three facing forward and three facing the rear. While better than third class, it still had the chickens, pigs, and goats.

On a visit to a church in Kafanchan, far to the north, I told Bible stories to the children in our compartment. Men, women, and children listened and asked questions. Nine years later I met a young man who had heard these stories on the train. He took his wife and children to church so they could hear the same stories. They all found the Lord and were serving Him faithfully. I remembered then that long trip — three days and two nights in the same position, my long legs drawn up, no room on the floor for my big feet; they were on boxes or bags of food. But the end of the journey made everything all right.

Dozens of people shouting the praises of God met me at Kafanchan. They knew that a missionary getting off the train in the multitude of passengers would hear their sounds of praise and be drawn to them. Sure enough, I found my people with big smiles and a great welcome that made me forget the hardships of travel.

These people far from their homeland had many problems. I listened, consoled, advised, and read the Scriptures to them for guidance or encouragement, for they endeavored to do the work of God faithfully.

The Kafanchan church had no qualified pastor. So they listened eagerly while I preached. And they remembered what they heard! Years later some could quote my text and give the points of my sermons.

The members worked long and hard, but they started their day with a 5:00 a.m. prayer meeting at their churches. Although I had come to teach them, they taught me many ways to serve God.

Altar Room for Idol Slaves

One evening our pastor brought three elderly strangers to me. They had walked two days from Eziama Oparanadim, a town 40 miles away. They had heard of how God had healed one of our members and said, "We have much sickness in our town. We have paid much money to our priests, but the sick people remain the same or even worse. Sir, we would like you to come and do for us what you have done in Umuahia."

Pastor James Nwaogbo told them about the Lord. As a result they built a "prayer house" for services and a house for the pastor who came at their request, to teach them. Many gave up their heathen customs and became real Christians. However, after six months no one had yet received the baptism in the Holy Spirit.

On a visit to Eziama Oparanadim, as usual I asked for questions after preaching. A man named Lazarus told me about a strong idol in their town. People from all around brought offerings to this god. When they were in trouble or afflicted with illness, they brought a child or a baby, as a living sacrifice to be a slave of the idol's priest. When these children were old enough, they married other slaves.

Now some of the idol-owned slaves had begun to attend the church. The "free-born" citizens didn't want any of these dirty, ragged, idol slaves in their church. "It spoils our good name," Lazarus said. "Why, they are even coming to the altar and seeking the baptism in the Holy Spirit." He asked me to forbid them to attend the church.

Following a good African custom, I told the people, "I'll study this matter, and we will talk it over on my next visit. In the meantime we will give them a small end of the altar where these slaves can pray." I drew a line on the mud altar and explained, "This part of the altar is for the slaves only."

About three months later I visited the Oparanadim church and preached about the slaves in Paul's day who had been saved and filled with the Holy Spirit. When I had delivered my sermon (which had been about three months in the making), I asked for questions.

My friend Lazarus stood up and said, "Sir, I have something to say. About thirty of us have received the Holy Spirit. And, Sir, do you know where I got the baptism? In that area you gave to the slaves. You see, the slaves began to receive the Holy Spirit. Then some of us decided that we would do anything to receive this experience. So, we went to the part of the altar that you gave to the slaves. Now many of our people have received the Holy Spirit; some in one area, some in another, and some at home. We found out what you said this morning, 'God is no respecter of persons.' "

These slaves were being persecuted by the heathen priests and badly beaten, but they continued to come to church in large numbers, even though they knew they would be flogged for it. I made an appeal on their behalf, but the government would not interfere in their customs and beliefs. When Nigeria got its independence this situation changed drastically. The slaves were given land and became free citizens also.

Years later I learned that the work had grown until there were seven churches in that area.

A Pastor With Leprosy?

God sometimes uses unusual means to take the gospel into certain areas. John Nwosu was a faithful young man who worked about a year for Elmer Frink. Then he went to Bible school and became a pastor. But shortly afterwards he discovered that he had leprosy! He was sent to the Uzuakoli Leprosy Settlement, a Methodist Mission project north of Umuahia.

Leprosy patients received daily injections of olmugo

oil. They were examined monthly. If a patient showed no evidence of leprosy for 12 months, doctors would declare him well and able to return to normal life in his community. After 12 months free from the symptoms, John was declared cured. A ceremony followed that included great thanksgiving by all — one of their number had been cured of leprosy!

The one unhappy man was John Nwosu as he went home. He was glad to be well but hated to leave. He had faithfully ministered the gospel among the 1,000 lepers. Hundreds had given their hearts to the Lord.

Shortly after John left, the British director of the settlement wrote requesting that he return as the pastor. It would provide his salary and a place for him and his family to live in the "clean" area. He could remain in the Assemblies of God and be free to minister according to his own convictions. John pastored there for many years until his death.

"That Man Doesn't Live Here."

On one visit to Gabriel Oyakhilome's area, he took me to a remote town that we reached after hours on bicycles. The people had never heard the gospel. No missionary had preached in that part of Nigeria. Some of the people had never even seen a white man.

The whole town gathered in the village square. Gabriel interpreted as I asked if they had ever heard of my friend Jesus or if they knew Him. The old men leaned their heads together and talked and talked. The rest of the people in small groups talked with frowns of concentration. Finally they said, "That man doesn't live in this town or in any of the towns around that we know about. In fact, the name doesn't sound like a man's name; it sounds more like a woman's name."

So I began with Adam and Eve and spoke of creation, sin, and sacrifice. I told them the story of Jesus Christ, the Savior of all men. When I finished they asked many questions about Jesus. Finally one said, "When did you hear about Jesus?"

"Oh," I said, "my mother taught me His name when I was a baby in her arms."

"So you have known Him all your life. You say this is good news that you are bringing us?"

"Yes."

"Where have you been all our lives? Why are we hearing about this just today? If this is such good news, why have we not heard it before today?"

They asked about my parents and grandparents. Had they known about Jesus? Then a very old man said, "Will you look at me? I am the oldest man in this town, and I am hearing this name 'Jesus' for the first time. Where have you been? Why didn't you come earlier?" All the counselors and people agreed — why were they hearing this story so late in their lives?

How do you answer such questions? I told them, "Gabriel Oyakhilome has brought me to tell you about Jesus so you can know Him too. Jesus will forgive your sins if you ask Him and accept Him as your Savior."

Eventually one old man said, "Sir, we are too old. Don't bother with us; we can't change. We give you the town and the people; we even give you our young people and children. Teach them."

So we tried to do just that and established churches in that area. I never heard of any of those men accepting Christ. I was in that town only once, but I have never been able to forget their question, "Where were you all our lives?" Others like them are dying in their sins without Christ; some have never heard His name. God help us to reach them!

CHAPTER TEN

"Write. . . Make It Plain!"

Guided by a Scrap of Paper

Jones Mkpah was getting ready for a fishing trip in the Bay of Benin in his large dugout canoe. Eight or ten men would haul long nets through the water for days until they had plenty of fish to sell. He hated to leave this time because his mother was very sick.

While walking along the shore, his eye fell on a scrap of paper. It was wet and sandy, part of a tract telling of God's love — a love so great that He would heal sick bodies. Jones knew nothing of this God. But, as the name and address in America of the writer was given, Jones wrote to him about his mother's illness.

He received an answer with the addresses of some of our missionaries. They visited Jones and his mother, and both became happy believers in the Lord.

This middle-aged man went to Bible school and became an apostle to the fishing villages along the ocean front, committed to "catching men" for Christ.

How did that scrap of paper get on the wet ocean sands? No one knows. Because one man found it, read it, and believed the printed word, hundreds of men and women were saved and little churches line that coast.

And the writer of the tract? I don't know his name, but somewhere in a book in heaven is his name and the full story of Jones Mkpah and the converts he won after reading a wet, sandy piece of a tract.

The Urgent Need

God's command to Habakkuk to write the vision and make it plain (Habakkuk 2:2) applied to our urgent need for literature in every phase of our work. A deep hunger for the Word of God accompanied the outpouring of the Spirit in the 1930's. The Church of England and Methodist missionaries had translated the Bible into Ibo and Efik, the languages in our area. But that was the full extent of available literature.

Many were just learning to read in English and in their own language. There was no simply written literature for them. The national church had begun literacy classes in the churches. In fact, some of the converts had to enroll in these classes before they could be baptized. While this requirement seemed strange to the missionaries, the national leaders knew the converts needed to read the Bible for themselves if they were to become overcoming Christians.

Rex Jackson felt deeply the need of regular Bible teaching in Sunday school. But there were no suitable materials. We used American quarterlies, but only the educated people and the pastors could read these. Besides, they were foreign to African culture.

Many of our good Bible school textbooks were not applicable to the culture. So, we decided to prepare studies especially for Africans, and print the notes on our Multigraph machine. And we needed tracts, songbooks, and other materials for evangelism and growth. Someone needed to give full time to writing.

Printing Presses and Journalism

Rex Jackson began to consider the possibility of starting our own Assemblies of God publishing house, but the equipment was not available. Two men in America learned of our need and gave us their printing presses and equipment.

But printing presses alone don't make publishing houses. Needing to write or edit, translate, and adapt materials, Rex went to a college in America in 1949 to get training in journalism and publishing.

Meanwhile, Lonnie Calloway, a new missionary and a printer, set up the first press and trained three young men to operate it (by foot — we had no electricity), and set the type. He built a print shop in Aba, on a corner next to our church. When the Jacksons returned, Rex took over the publishing.

From English to Ibo

Rex had started writing Sunday school lessons in simple, African-oriented English. These were our first project. But most people could read only their native language. Several pastors who spoke excellent English translated the quarterlies into Ibo. We were surprised to see the spiritual growth that resulted. The Christians devoured the lessons, absorbing truths that helped them withstand temptation and persecution.

We saw the success of our literature program in a two-week, interdenominational training program for workers in the 1950 campaign with Billy Graham. Only those passing the exam were to be personal workers. Assemblies of God members from two churches were over half of those who passed the exam. They had already learned most of the material in Sunday school lessons.

Reaching Out With Literature

Soon we were printing tracts, booklets, and other literature in English and in the vernacular. We began a bookshop to sell Bibles and other supplies. But the bookshop reached only those who came to it. So Rex got a vending trailer with sides that opened up. He pulled it to markets and reached more people with the Word.

The literacy level had risen greatly, and the people had a great desire for something to read. Courses by correspondence were very popular. And so, literature was an important part of evangelism and church growth.

Esther Cimino, helpers, and correspondence courses

Our church in Aba entered an international Sunday school contest in 1956. It had an average attendance of 125. The members set a goal of 600 by October. In April they started going from door to door giving out tracts explaining the church's beliefs and inviting people to come to Sunday school during the contest.

Curious townspeople didn't wait until October. Before then, the church had passed its goal of 600.

During the contest, the church rented big trucks and brought the first load of people, filling the building and the church yard. After Sunday school, they took these home and brought a second and a third group. More than 2500 people came each Sunday for six weeks.

Ten of our churches entered this interdenominational contest. In divisions according to their size: Enugu won second prize; Aba, third; two rural schools, fourth and fifth; and three, honorable mention. Seven out of ten were winners in a world-wide competition!

Christians in Aba continued their evangelistic efforts, and when there was no room the church divided to form more congregations. Today there are over 50 Assemblies of God churches in Aba and its suburbs. The original Sunday school averages over 2,000, the result in part of the distribution of literature.

Continued Growth

Soon Sunday school lessons were translated into Efik, and then into Hausa, Ishan, Egedde, and Yoruba as the work spread throughout Nigeria into the Muslim North, the Midwest, the interior, and Western Nigeria.

As the evangelistic program grew it demanded more literature. Two other missionaries, Monroe Robison and Andrew Hargrave gave their time mainly to printing. With the coming of electricity, motors on the presses sped up production. A typesetting machine was a great improvement! Publishing gospel literature, now totally under the management of nationals, still contributes to church growth and the stability of the believers.

From original to modern equipment

CHAPTER ELEVEN

When Afraid... Trust

A Man-Eating Leopard

All the large wild animals had been killed off in Pastor David Anyim's area. But suddenly tragedy struck. A man-eating leopard stalked its prey in and around their village. It had probably wandered down from northern Nigeria after becoming too old to catch antelope and had turned to killing easier prey — people. In two months this leopard killed 56 people.

One day Mrs. Anyim and her daughter were going to the river for water. Suddenly the leopard stepped into the path in front of them. Mrs. Anyim pushed her daughter behind her and stood paralyzed with fear.

That morning in the prayer meeting, she had been led to pray for safety. Now, suddenly she was mightily moved by the Holy Spirit and began to shout in an unknown language. The leopard glared at her, then it sprang into the bush and was gone. Mother and child went on safely. The next day the leopard was killed.

God protected His people as they faced many kinds of danger. Courageous Christians pressed into Satan's territory with the gospel. And, like the psalmist, when afraid they put their trust in the Lord.

"No Christians Allowed"

The town of Ntalakwu had a large banner across the main road: "No Christians Allowed".. Anyone who came to witness knew that danger awaited him. Some of our Christians in a nearby town took up the challenge. The pastor started holding outdoor services there, usually with a group of men, but sometimes alone. The women went as a group, visiting the women. They handed out tracts, prayed for the sick, and showed their love.

After months of ministry, the pastor and a group of men went to the chief and asked for land on which to build a church. He denied their request. Again and again they repeated it as the number of converts grew. Finally he gave them a poor piece of land.

The Christians from the towns round about, together with those in the village, gathered the materials needed and built the church. Then it was time for a pastor to be appointed. The pastor who started the work usually had a group with him. It would be more dangerous to lived among those who threatened that their village would never have a Christian church.

I discussed the matter with the students in Bible school. One man offered to be the pastor there. After he moved to Ntalakwu, he knew his life was in danger, but daily he held services in the church for the few who were brave enough to attend. One by one, others accepted the Lord until there was a strong church. The heathen leaders saw they had lost the battle and took the banner down. That church opened others in all the area around it. God was with them, daily adding to their number those who were being saved.

Cloth and Christ to Egedde

Paul Oji, a member of the Aba assembly, was a successful trader, selling cloth. Carrying it, covered with plastic, on the back of his bicycle, he would travel till he found a market with little cloth. Then he would rent a space and set up his business.

One day Paul learned of a tribe in the interior of the

Northern Region, where there were few traders and cloth was scarce. This tribe spoke Egedde, but "pidgin" English was used in all the markets and Paul knew it. So, he went by train to the station nearest to Egedde and the rest of the way on his bicycle.

Everywhere Paul went he took literature and witnessed to the people while selling his cloth. One day as he was pedaling his bicycle into the mountains to the markets of Egedde, God spoke to him, "Paul, what do you have with you besides the cloth?"

"Lord, I have my cloth, my Bible, and some tracts that I will distribute as I sell my cloth," Paul replied. He was then strongly impressed to preach in the markets. Paul couldn't speak Egedde, but he spoke in Ibo and English to those around him.

One day, a young man said, "My name is Moses Onda, and I belong to these people. I understand Ibo also." From then on Paul preached and Moses interpreted, even though Moses was not a Christian.

The Lord dealt with Moses as he interpreted the message of salvation. When Paul gave the invitation to repent and be saved, Moses was one of the first to respond. During the following months God used these two young men mightily among the Egedde people.

One day Paul Oji appeared at the Bible school, bringing Moses with him, and applied for admission. Moses couldn't speak English. But Paul interceded for him, promising to teach him English and help him with his assignments. So, both were accepted.

At the end of the school term, they continued their ministry in Egedde. They came back to school, and in the first service Moses was filled with the Spirit. What a change this made in him! Now he felt definitely called to preach Christ to his people.

To Be or Not to Be a Chief?

Moses Onda and Andrew Odimbar faced the same life-determining decision while in Bible school. Andrew knew his Bible better than most pastors and quoted many portions from it in his preaching. He was a man of the Word, a happy, wonderfully spirited young man with a beautiful family. His future seemed bright although, like all of our pastors, he was very poor.

One day in Andrew's senior year he disappeared. The students told me that the elders had come from his town to take him to be the chief of their clan at Ntalakwu. His uncle, who had been their chief and had no sons, had died. Andrew, as the oldest nephew, was his heir. He would be rich, inheriting the fine house, farmlands, and the many wives of his uncle.

But he would have to become the spiritual leader of a heathen clan! This meant going from serving God to serving idols, sacrificing to idols for himself, his family, and all his clan. This young man gave up the things of eternity for those of the moment!

Several times when I was in that area, I went by Andrew's house hoping to visit him. His people always told me, "Sir, he is not at home." He was embarrassed and had given the word that he would not see me.

One day I received word that the chief of Ntalakwu had died. Andrew's people buried him with all the heathen customs. My wonderful friend who loved the Word of God and knew it so well had succumbed to temptation, lost his soul, died as a heathen! What sorrow such losses bring to any missionary's heart!

Moses Onda, from the Egedde people, faced an identical temptation. Elders from his village came to Robert Cobb, director of the Bible school at that time, and said, "We have come to take our chief." Paul Oji and Moses Onda were interpreting. Paul explained that Moses had been chosen chief of Egedde and the elders had come to escort him back to their tribe.

Moses said, "The men in my family have been chiefs for many years. My uncle was sick when I came to school, and they tell me he died. Brother Cobb, please tell me what to do."

"Moses, this is a decision you must make. I can't make it for you. But we can ask God for guidance," explained Brother Cobb. So he earnestly prayed.

A long silence followed. Then Moses stood before the men in deference to their age and spoke kindly of his feelings for them. But, as he had become a Christian, he could not be their chief. He declared to all, "I want to be a follower of Jesus, and I want to preach the gospel." Moses had made his decision. The elders were not happy as he explained his determination to preach the gospel when he returned to their village.

When school was out, Moses and Paul went back to Egedde. But this time things were different. The village elders whose offer Moses had rejected refused to give him permission for a church in his village. So he went outside the village and built a church, which was promptly burned down by the heathen chief. Everything that Moses owned was destroyed in that fire. He suffered much and was beaten. But he would not give up his determination to preach the gospel.

Moses returned to Bible school and graduated, selected as class speaker. God blessed the ministry of this young man who refused an earthly kingdom to become a preacher. Persecution became worse, but God's work grew. Twenty years later there were 40 churches in that tribe. Fourteen Egedde pastors had graduated from Bible school, men called by God as a result of the example and preaching of Paul Oji and Moses Onda.

Kenneth Godbey, our nearest missionary, told us about climbing the mountains to reach Egedde, in some places so steep that he went up on hands and knees. After resting at the top he went on the weary miles to the village where Moses was waiting. People came by the hundreds. The believers, townspeople, and even the chiefs came to hear Kenneth preach. His visit encouraged the pastors and made their life easier, as the chiefs saw that a mission was behind them.

Years later a road was built over the mountains and visitors were amazed at the growth of the work.

Paul Oji was killed in a motorcycle accident, and Moses Onda went to be with the Lord after a short illness. But they had built on a solid foundation. And this work has continued to grow through the years.

Mammy Water or Christ?

Sunday Aaron, a teacher in our school at Aba, began to think of his people, the Ogoni tribe. They were fishermen in a part of the Niger River Delta where we had never gone. The chief would not allow a church to be built, because the tribe was dedicated to Mammy Water, Goddess of the Sea. Sunday explained:

"Every person takes an oath never to serve any other god. They seal that oath with their blood. In the ceremony, the witch doctor cuts their arms, catches the blood, and mixes it with sea water. Then each one drinks a little of this mixture. Should one break this oath, it would bring disaster on the whole tribe in the minds of the chief and the people."

Sunday knew that the head chief would refuse to let any mission settle among the 250,000 Ogonis. But he begged the pastor to go there, preach, and start a church. They came to us in Port Harcourt; and Dorothy, Donald, and I went with them to Dere, Sunday's town, and met his family. Their house was too small for a service, but a neighbor let us use his living room.

Sunday went all around town inviting people to a meeting — what kind of meeting, he didn't tell them! While I gave a simple gospel message to a packed house, a court messenger handed a note in through the window. Sunday was greatly disturbed. He said, "The chief has asked you to meet him in the town square."

The pastor said, "This chief is a very rough man. He won't be happy about the service we have had."

Our family, the pastor, Sunday, and about 50 others waited an hour in the square. Finally the chief appeared in his fancy regalia. He would not speak with us but handed us a note stating: "I do not want you to return to this town again. We do not want a mission or church among the Ogoni people; I will not have it. A missionary came here ten years ago. I had my young men meet him outside of town, where they flogged him. He has never been back." This was my warning.

A few days later the pastor sent me word that Sunday had disappeared. On the evening of that service in Ogoni, after we had left, the chief gathered up all who had been in the service — men, women, children, and the owner of the house — and had put them in jail. Some were there six months before they were released with a warning never to have another service of this kind.

I knew that the laws of Nigeria guaranteed religious freedom, so I went alone directly to the chief's house. When a little servant boy came to the door, I said, "I want to see the chief." He sent word that he didn't want to see me. I said, "I want you to tell the chief that I will be back, and we will have a service, even though some in the first one were put in jail. We are going to have another service." Then I added, "Be sure to tell him that on my way here I talked with the district officer. I am here with his permission. I am going to have a service."

A man who knew pidgin English interpreted for me. (Others were more capable, but were afraid.) We had an outdoor service. Even as I spoke I knew that about 30 people were still in jail because of that first service. And no one knew what had happened to Sunday.

I returned to Ogoni several times, sometimes with the pastor and Ogoni converts from Aba who interpreted for me, sometimes alone. I never saw the chief again.

Several people accepted Christ. At last three converts were ready for water baptism, among them one of the chief's counselors. When I arrived for the baptismal service Sunday, I heard crying and wailing. The chief's counselor who was to have been baptized had been invited to dinner by the chief Saturday evening. He had died in agony early the next morning, evidently poisoned. We went ahead and baptized the other two converts. It was a subdued occasion.

About that time some of the lady missionaries were going to teach a course in homemaking at the Bible school. We went to Ogoni in and took two carloads of young women to Umuahia for two weeks of classes and wonderful meetings. Some were saved, and some received the baptism in the Holy Spirit.

For nine months no one knew what had happened to Sunday. Then on a trip to the Midwest Area, about 600 miles from Ogoni, I sent word ahead to announce my visit in two or three newspapers. I stayed at the Midwest Bible school while in that area.

Sunday Aaron saw the announcement of my coming, sold his shoes for money to ride part of the way in a truck, then walked the last 15 miles. He had fled from Ogoni for his life, knowing the chief would kill him for having taken me there to preach. He was afraid to let his wife know that he was alive, afraid the chief would kill her and their children.

I arranged for him to go back to Umuahia and live at the Bible school until we knew it was safe for him to go home. Two of the lady missionaries drove to Ogoni and brought his wife and children back with them. How happy she was! Sunday enrolled in Bible school and became a real blessing there, teaching English.

Some months later I returned to America to become the Field Secretary for the Assemblies of God in Africa. After I had been gone about a year, two carloads of missionaries went to the Ogoni area. Under the same tree where I had been warned never to return, they held a big service.

In the middle of the service, who do you think came and sat down on the front row? The chief, in all his finery and with his counselors! Rex Jackson, knowing his history, preached with all his heart. When Rex gave the invitation to accept Christ, the chief responded! How I would have loved to be there! A few months later I received a letter signed by the chief: "Reverend, Sir: First I want to beg your forgiveness for threatening your life on that first visit you made to our town. Forgive me, for I did not know what I was doing. Today I have many enemies since I have become a Christian. Pray for me that I may be faithful.

"I have been sick, very sick, and I fear that my days may be few. Please, when you visit Nigeria, come to my house. Then we can go to church together."

In my visits to Nigeria, I was never able to go back to Ogoni. So I never saw the chief again, who was now my friend. He has gone to be with the Lord, so we will meet together in the presence of Christ.

God wonderfully used Lillian Bach in Ogoni. In 1959 simple buildings had been erected in Dere and a school was opened with 80 women and girls enrolled.

Sunday Aaron graduated from Bible school and returned to his people to preach and to lead the work. In 1986 he wrote telling how God was blessing. Many towns and villages had been touched by his ministry and churches were established. He was the principal of a new territorial Bible school. Sunday had once run for his life, but came back and faced the persecution, and God had blessed his family and his ministry.

CHAPTER TWELVE

"Commit to Faithful Men"

Left: Executive Presbytery, 1964: Gabriel Oyakhilome, I. Ogbuagu, Matthew Ezeigbo, Rex Jackson, Will Woko, Roland Ohirhia, Godwin Akwarandu
Right: Superintendent Charles O. Osueke, 1988

Working With National Leaders

When Lloyd Shirer and the Church of Jesus Christ founded the Assemblies of God of Nigeria in 1939, they established cooperative leadership. When I became superintendent in 1940, all my work was in cooperation with the Nigerian leaders in the Executive Committee. George Alioha was Assistant Superintendent.

As the work grew, district presbyters supervised the work in each area. They appointed Bible school students to the small churches that were springing up.

The pastors taught a class for new converts to train them in God's Word. At examination time for the section, the presbyter tested them. Prospective members explained from the Bible what salvation is, and told what had taken place in their lives, what they had done with their idols and jujus, what their family felt about their conversion. This process was slow, but the leaders explained that people born again out of heathenism might retain some heathen practices without knowing the seriousness of continuing them.

Our national leaders had reason to be careful. In the great Pentecostal revival, the lack of spiritual leaders had brought a rise of false prophets and charlatans who baptized heathen men and women by the hundreds for a shilling apiece. Some taught that sins were washed away in baptism. When the time was set for a baptismal service, they warned the people downstream to get their drinking water before that hour. After all, who would want to drink another person's sins?

When some independent churches ran into trouble, some wanted to affiliate with us. To our sorrow, we accepted a few of them. Our leaders had problems in trying to impose scriptural doctrine and practice, because the people were already set in their teachings and practices. Their pastors opposed Bible school training. So, we decided not to receive such churches into our fellowship.

National Superintendents

The executive committee labored faithfully in the development of the work. The superintendent was chairman. Missionaries who have served in this capacity are: Lloyd Shirer (for six months), Everett Phillips, Clarence Goudie, Elmer Frink, Rex Jackson, Harry Pennington, and Robert Carlson.

Since 1961 Nigerian leaders and a representative of the missionaries have formed the executive committee. Matthew Ezeigbo was elected then as superintendent. He had proved himself worthy as a pastor, Director of Good News Crusades and Evangelism, Bible school teacher, General Treasurer, District Superintendent, and Assistant General Superintendent.

Matthew had heard God audibly call him to full-time ministry while he was Chief Steward at Kingsway Stores. From that time on he had dedicated his life and service to the Lord. God uniquely shaped his life to lead a church that touched about 30 tribes. His wife was an excellent aid to his ministry. Stella was a great leader and a godly example to all the women.

In 1971 Gabriel Oyakhilome was elected as General Superintendent. He was the first convert in a large area of central Nigeria and the first pastor of his tribe of Ishan. He became the superintendent of the newly formed Midwest District. God's touch was evident on him as he labored in this capacity until elected General Superintendent. He served with distinction in this office until his retirement.

Matthew Ezeigbo was again elected in 1982 and served until his retirement in 1988. At that time Charles O. Osueke became the superintendent.

In half a century God has blessed the Assemblies of God in Nigeria until today it is the largest active Protestant church in this nation. Such growth could never have taken place without the type of spiritual leadership given by the Nigerian superintendents and other officials in the national organization

Secrets of Success

Frequently people have questioned me about the success of God's work in Nigeria, the ever-growing number of churches, the work of the Nigerian leaders, and how such a work was financed. Part has been due to the systematic training in God's Word (we owe much to those who came before us and translated it into the major languages), the close cooperation among the missionaries and national ministers, and the dedicated labors of all.

I know God has a plan, and we have tried to follow it from the first, for a self-supporting, self-governing, and self-propagating church in every country — "the indigenous church." Today Nigerians are building their churches, paying their pastors, and conducting the church programs with their own funds.

The work of God in Nigeria would not be what it is today if it were not for hundreds of dedicated pastors, evangelists, and teachers. Some have been beaten, their houses burned, their property stolen, their children dismissed from school — all for the gospel's sake. They have gone hungry and suffered in other ways for the cause of Christ. They have opened hundreds of churches and done exploits in His name.

But the most important secret of success is the outpouring of the Holy Spirit upon the people. Dorothy and I are humbly grateful for the visitation and power of the Holy Spirit. He made the work what it is today.

The Unfinished Task

A half completed masterpiece by Raphael was carried in his funeral cortege. Schubert left his "Unfinished Symphony." History is filled with such stories — a life too short, a task unfinished.

Nearly two thousand years ago a young man died at the age of thirty-three The sick had been healed, the blind saw, and the common people heard Him, gained hope and believed. He died after three short years of service. Why should He have died at such an early age?

But remember Christ's words: "It is finished!" The will of God for His life on earth was gloriously finished at Calvary. What appeared an unfinished task had a glorious culmination in a bloody cross, a body torn by rough iron spikes — and an empty tomb!

The apostle Paul could say, "I have fought a good fight, I have finished my course, I have kept the faith." There were vast areas still untouched with Christ's message, yet Paul had a divinely given sense of having completed what God had given him to do.

God's program of redemption, in progress ever since sin entered the world, will be finished just as He has planned. Sin will be defeated. The "kingdoms of this world shall become the kingdoms of our Lord and of His Christ." The world shall be restored to its original pristine beauty. Jesus shall reign!

Our share in this great program is to complete our part, fulfill God's will for us as individuals. The early home-going of one of His saints always seems a tragedy. But the real tragedy lies in a man's life wasted-opportunities squandered and talents buried.

Today as I write, my thoughts are of my son, cut down by a heart attack at a young age. Ever since God called him into His service, Don's chief desire was to teach in an overseas Bible college. He was doing that in Holland. Was his task finished?

And what of my task — that purpose which God directed from the time of my conversion and even before? What of God's divine program for your life? With no fixed guarantees of next year, and only today assured us, let us work while it is today. "The night is coming when no man can work."

Epilogue
— *Rex Jackson*

"A man's life is his most enduring monument."

I don't know who first said this, but it could never be applied more truly than to Everett L. Phillips. Throughout Africa's most populous nation, Nigeria, and in other countries of that continent many can witness to the influence of his life and ministry. I was privileged to start my 40 years of missionary service under the guidance of Brother Phillips in Nigeria. A fellowship developed between us that meant more than I can ever say. His dedication, his wisdom, his love for Africa all inspired me and helped establish in me a philosophy of missions that contributed to the success of God's work in that land.

After serving as field secretary for Africa for 17 years, he retired in March 1971. He and his wife pastored in Venice, Florida, for two years. Then they returned to Springfield, Missouri, where Brother Phillips served as an associate minister of Central Assembly of God for six years. Although he suffered from heart problems and was not so active after this, he continued to bless the steady stream of friends, former co-workers, and young people who visited the Phillips' home at Maranatha Village.

A few months after completing the initial draft of this book, Brother Phillips was called to his eternal reward on January 12, 1988. He has gone on to be with the Lord, but his life continues to inspire and encourage a host of those following in his steps.

ASSEMBLIES OF GOD OF NIGERIA, 1988

Ministers: 2,887	Layworkers: 734
Missionaries: 17	Churches: 3,052
Outstations: 250	Adherents: 542,688
Bible Schools: 8	Enrollment: 1,223

ASSEMBLIES OF GOD MISSIONARIES IN NIGERIA

Years in Nigeria	Missionaries	Other Fields
1939-44, 51-54	Everett & Dorothy Phillips	All of Africa
1941-65	Rex Jackson	Togo, ICI, Literature
1945-65	Martha Jackson	
1941-49	Elmer Frink	
1944-49	Betty Hall Frink	
1943-77	Kenneth & Geraldine Godbey	Germany, ICI
1944-50	Clarence & Gladys Goudie	
1944-46	James & Maybelle Hance	
1944-57, 73-79	Cledith Cox	Malawi
1944-84	Minnie Ecklund	
1945-54	Dorothy Buck (Goudie)	Ghana
1945-86	Martha Jacobson (Bauer)	
1945-56	Mathilda Birkland	
1945-83	Lillian Bach	
1945-57	Harry & Eva Shumway	
1945-49	Lloyd & Ruby Aud	
1946-57	Elsie Weber	
1946-48	Cornelius & Mildred Van Dalen	
1946-81	Irene Crane	
1946-80	May Garner	
1948-72	Ralph & Velma Cobb	
1948-57	Paul & Helen Bruton	Benin, Tanzania
1948-53	Lonnie & Stella Calloway	Lesotho

1949-51	David & Claudia Wakefield	Togo-Benin, Senegal
1950-62	Robert & Naomi Cobb	Tanzania, Ghana, S.Africa
1951-75	Harry & Miriam Pennington	Zaire
1951-79	Miriam Pennington	
1952-57	Raymond & Lynita Brock	
1953-61	Jeanet Wimberly	Liberia
1955-82	David & Lois McCulley	Liberia
1954-	Ralph & Esther Cimino	
1954-65	Charles & Gwenyth Lee	
1955-69	Walter & Elsie Kornelson	Sierra Leone, S.Africa
1956-71	Andrew & Doris Hargrave	Ghana, Costa Rica
1956-69	Florence Metcalf	Malawi
1957-69	Robert & Margaret Carlson	Europe, Belgium, S.Africa, ICI
1957-63	James & Inga King	Liberia, Togo-Benin
1958-64	Ward & Twila Woods	Ghana, Upper Volta
1959-82	Phyllis Wagner	Kenya
1959-63	Carol Elaine Wingren	
1960-63	Melvin & Verna Grams	S.Africa, Liberia, Europe, ICI
1960-69	Monroe & Marie Robison	Ghana, Life Publishers
1961-71, 75-77	Gerald & Maxine Falley	Liberia, Ghana
1961-69	Donald & Theola Phillips	S.Africa, Holland
1961-88	Robert & Dorothy Webb	ICI Belgium
1963-67	Bernard & Elsie Bresson	
1963-65	Raymond & Bernita Mae Lockwood	
1963-84	Martha Underwood	Kenya
1963-85	Doris Geiger (Peterson)	
1964-73	Glenn & LaVerda Reeves	
1965-	Ruby Peterson	

INDEX OF PICTURES

A.G.D.S
ASSEMBLIES OF GOD DIVINITY SCHOOL
OF NIGERIA
Africa's largest protestant Bible college

When Everett Phillips started what was then Central Bible Institute in Umuahia, Nigeria, little did he or anyone else imagine the impact it would make on the growth of the Nigeria Assemblies of God. Today, more than 500 Nigerian men and women attend A.G.D.S. in diploma and degree level programs. Now known as the *Assemblies of God Divinity School,* it is the "centerpiece" of a network of eight Assemblies of God Bible schools across Nigeria.

Nearly 1300 students attend these schools, and every year many graduate to start churches, lead thriving congregations, evangelize, and teach God's Word. These schools are the seedbed of the growth of the Nigeria Assemblies of God to over half a million believers in more than 3000 churches.

A.G.D.S. must build to keep up with growth. There is no choice. Right now a new student dormitory building is going up. It will cost at least $250,000. Added administrative and office facilities plus other buildings must follow to handle present and future growth.

What better way to honor the memory of Everett Phillips than through a gift to the growth of A.G.D.S., Africa's largest Protestant Bible school? It cannot stop. It must grow if the Church is to reach *Africa's most populous nation for Christ!* Everett Phillips' vision must go on

Farewell

On his farewell visit to Nigeria in 1970 Everett Phillips received a letter of appreciation from a young pastor who in 1988 would become superintendent of the Assemblies of God of Nigeria. After referring to the personal encouragement and wise counsel he had received, Charles O. Osueke wrote:

> "I am one of those thousands of African workers to whom your life and ministry have been a great blessing and encouragement. Your devotion to duty involving personal sacrifice of time and leisure has once and again sent me to my knees, where I lay my all at the feet of Jesus to fulfill the great cause whereunto He has called me.

> "I hate to think of a possible permanent parting with you here below. I am, nevertheless, consoled in the fact that we are destined to meet again somewhere, someday. If no more here under the sun, there at Jesus' feet where we meet to part no more I hope to look full into your face once more and thank you for the rich blessings you were to me on earth."

A great host of us echo the sentiments of Charles Osueke. For years I have counted it a great privilege to have Dorothy and Everett Phillips as my close neighbors and dear friends. Thank you, Everett, for blessing us all with your memories of Nigeria.

— Louise Jeter Walker